GEN. THEO. SEMINARY
LIBRARY
NEW YORK

JAMES LLOYD BRECK, D.D.

# An Apostle of the Wilderness

James Lloyd Breck, D.D.
His Missions and His Schools

By
THEODORE I. HOLCOMBE, B.D.

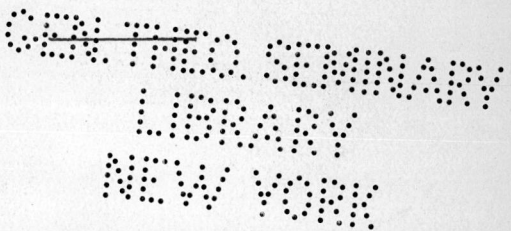

NEW YORK
THOMAS WHITTAKER
2 AND 3 BIBLE HOUSE
1903

Copyright, 1903,
By Thomas Whittaker

*To my beloved Wife
This book is dedicated*

# Preface

THE writer has long felt that the time would come when in a good conscience he ought to publish his contribution to the life history of James Lloyd Breck, D. D.

Dr. Breck has already found a chronicler in the person of his brother, who survived him, the Rev. Charles Breck, D. D., whose book was published some twenty years ago, but is now almost out of print. I wish to express here my sense of obligation to this life of Dr. Breck for information and assistance in the preparation of this book.

My reason for these personal reminiscences is found in the fact that I am the only person now living who can speak for that particular time; from 1849 to 1852: which covered the period when the mission at St. Paul and the Indian field were founded.

With these explanations and acknowledgments this imperfect volume is committed to that generous but discriminating public from whose verdict there is no appeal.

THE AUTHOR.

# Introductory

WHEN the world needs a man, the man appears. Extraordinary occasions require unusual men. This is so evident in history, that all men recognize the man when he appears. I think I am safe in saying that the American Catholic Church has furnished no man of the type of James Lloyd Breck since its foundation. When, after Dr. Breck's death, the Bishop of Pittsburg said in his convention address, "That it was hard to think of the Church without James Lloyd Breck in it," he expressed a fact which all men at the time realized. Here was a man who had captured the attention of all churchmen of the time in which he lived. He was known from the Atlantic to the Pacific, from the Lakes to the Gulf. His name was everywhere familiar, a household word, "a burning and a shining light," that never grew dim or obscure for thirty-five long years. He was twenty-two years of age when he left New York for Wisconsin, and fifty-seven when he died in Benicia, California, in 1877; and all that time he never took what we call a vacation, nor let up in the ardor of his strenuous life. In the true sense of the word he was a missionary—one sent to accomplish a definite work who could always say with the Master, Christ, "How am I straitened until it be accomplished." With St. Paul his motto was, "This one thing I do," and all he did he did with his might. Dr. Breck early realized that money was essential to his work, and to the securing of this necessity he devoted himself with the same zeal and perseverance that characterized all his work of a more spiritual character. How he endured the strain of it no one can tell. There are men of the clergy to-day who will say, "you cannot get money by writing." Dr. Breck had no such teacher in his time to whom he gave heed, or he had never accomplished his purposes, and so it was that "he found the pen mightier than the sword." Before him there was none like him and since his day none have arisen to fill his place. Men who have a mission are inspired men. We do well to reverence their memories. They are examples of heroic endeavor to their fellows in the battle of life, raised up for this very thing. They stand for a new awakening. They set in motion new agencies. They open up new paths for others to follow. They create a new epoch. They are apostles of a new era, and therefore we do them reverence, recognizing in them the "*divine gift*" men call genius. These men care not for wealth, nor fame, nor honors. They are God's men, who work for Him and with Him, and whether they understand it all like St. Paul, or work for selfish ends like Nebuchadnezzar in their ignorance, yet are they fulfilling a necessary work in the all encompassing plans of God, who maketh even the wrath of man to praise him. James Lloyd Breck created a new era in giving for missions. He smote the rock, and since that day the waters have continued to flow without abatement to irrigate the thirsty fields, that they should bring forth fruit to the glory of God and the upbuilding of His kingdom throughout the world. The General Convention of 1835 resolved " that every man by his baptism is a missionary," and it was ordained that in the life of James Lloyd Breck should be given to the world an illustration of what a missionary life could be. Such a life no one had yet seen on this continent. In the divine purpose he was to set out for the west to establish associate missions, to found universities, to plant schools for young women, to convert the Indians from their idolatries, and all this he was to do in faith, for all things were possible to him that believed. Such a man was James Lloyd Breck, unknown yet well known, silent of speech yet eloquent of works, alert, watchful, patient, uncomplaining, strenuous, courageous, prayerful and all things to all men that he might win some. He fought the good fight and kept the faith. He gave all he had until he gave his life an offering on the altar of duty. As he came into the world empty handed, so he left it, but better and brighter for his presence and richer in his example and his work. This life sketch is an humble tribute from one who knew and loved him for a space of thirty years.

T. I. H.

# Contents

|     |     |     |
| --- | --- | --- |
| I. | EARLY LIFE | 1 |
| II. | WISCONSIN | 7 |
| III. | NASHOTAH | 12 |
| IV. | NASHOTAH—CONTINUED | 19 |
| V. | NASHOTAH—IN 1847 | 26 |
| VI. | DIVERSITIES OF LABOR | 31 |
| VII. | A RELIGIOUS HOUSE | 35 |
| VIII. | JAMES LLOYD BRECK | 40 |
| IX. | THE JOURNEY TO ST. PAUL | 48 |
| X. | THE ASSOCIATE MISSION IN ST. PAUL | 56 |
| XI. | THE ASSOCIATE MISSION IN ST. PAUL—CONTINUED | 62 |
| XII. | THE JOURNEY TO THE INDIAN MISSION | 69 |
| XIII. | THE INDIAN MISSION | 76 |
| XIV. | THE INDIAN MISSION—CONTINUED | 81 |
| XV. | A CANOE TRIP | 85 |
| XVI. | THE PROVIDENTIAL MAN | 91 |
| XVII. | THE MARRIAGE OF DR. BRECK | 97 |
| XVIII. | THE TRYING YEAR | 101 |
| XIX. | ST. COLUMBA | 106 |
| XX. | KAHSAHGAH | 113 |

## Contents

| | | |
|---|---|---:|
| XXI. | Travels and Discoveries | 118 |
| XXII. | The Intelligence of the Indian | 123 |
| XXIII. | The New Mission | 128 |
| XXIV. | The New Mission—Continued | 132 |
| XXV. | "Wars and Rumors of Wars" | 137 |
| XXVI. | Enmegahbowh and the Indian War | 141 |
| XXVII. | Sioux and Ojibways | 147 |
| XXVIII. | Faribault | 150 |
| XXIX. | The Hall of Fame | 155 |
| XXX. | Ways and Means | 162 |
| XXXI. | California | 169 |
| XXXII. | Influence and Death of Dr. Breck | 176 |
| XXXIII. | The Burial at Benicia | 181 |
| XXXIV. | Twenty Years After | 184 |
| | Poem Read at the Funeral— "An Apostle of the Wilderness," | 190 |
| | Addenda | 193 |

# Illustrations

|  | PAGE |
|---|---|
| JAMES LLOYD BRECK, D.D. | *Frontispiece* |
| RT. REV. JACKSON KEMPER, D.D. | 14 |
| NASHOTAH IN 1847 | 26 |
| WILLIAM ADAMS, D.D. | 39 |
| "ENMEGAHBOWH" | 91 |
| ST. COLUMBA. FIRST INDIAN HOUSE WEST OF THE MISSISSIPPI RIVER | 106 |
| "POK-O-NAK-E-SHIK"—(HOLE-IN-THE-DAY)—INDIAN CHIEF | 141 |
| MONUMENT ERECTED AT NASHOTAH, 1898 | 190 |

# An Apostle of the Wilderness

## CHAPTER I

### EARLY LIFE

JAMES LLOYD BRECK was the fourth child in a family of fifteen children, born in the county of Philadelphia, Pa. His parents were George Breck and Catherine D'isreali his wife—of the island of Jamaica, W. I. Until his thirteenth year, James Lloyd lived on the family estate—attending the school of the neighborhood, and learning the general work of a farmer. About this time his uncle the Hon. James Lloyd died in Boston and left his namesake in his will $1,000. It was determined with this sum to send Lloyd to Dr. Muhlenberg's school at Flushing, L. I., where he remained for three years until the $1,000 was exhausted, when his aunt, Mrs. James Lloyd, sent him to the University of Pennsylvania, from which he graduated with honor at the end of two years.

While at Flushing, James Lloyd was distinguished for his industry and perseverance, and when he left there for the University, at sixteen years of age, he had already decided to enter the ministry if found worthy of so exalted a vocation. Thenceforth all his energies were consecrated to the fitting of himself for that sacred calling. Dr. Muhlenberg writes of him, "James is an excellent boy, his persevering industry, amiable disposition, and I may also add consistent piety afford gratifying promise that the wishes of his parents and instructors will not be disappointed; we have not a more industrious boy in the institute."

This is rare commendation, when we recall the eminent men of National reputation who were his associates, such as Odenheimer, Bedell, Kerfoot, Mahan, the two Passmores, James J. Biddle, Geo. W. Hunter and others. Of all these, none excelled James Lloyd Breck in industry. His light seemed always burning, in the small hours of the night, or the early dawn, and the same intense industry attended all his after life, until the light burned out on the shore of the Western ocean.

When James Lloyd entered the General Theological Seminary, at eighteen years of age, he found himself in the class of which Azel D. Cole and William Adams were members—a class of twenty-six, many of whom were distinguished in after years—and all of whom enjoyed the distinguished honor of having Dr. Whittingham as their spiritual adviser and example. Young Breck in his letters deplores the loss to the Seminary

## Early Life

when the great Doctor was chosen to become the Bishop of Maryland. In one of his letters to his uncle, we first hear of Mr. Adams from Dublin "as an Irishman possessed of their very quick parts in no small degree." In the same letter he declares, "he has so learned to make his bed that it holds its form in good shape for a whole week."

It was while in the Seminary that Bishop Kemper came and made his appeal for men to give themselves to the work of Christ in the wilderness of the West. To this appeal, the chivalrous spirit of Breck at once responded. Altogether there were eight who expressed themselves ready to go, at first, but finally the number dwindled to four, viz., Miles and Hobart, Breck and Adams. Then Miles, his Bishop objecting, dropped out, and there remained but three when the time set for the journey arrived.

The association of these young men at the Seminary for prayer and devotion, reminds one of John Wesley and his brother Charles, at Oxford, when religion was very low in England. These young men had a special service of their own—which had the approval of Bishop Whittingham, and in which they united on the Wednesday of each week.

This in itself set them apart as men who were waiting to be called to some special work, and it was only a question of what that work should be.

That young Breck had early settled his call to the ministry is very evident from the following letter to his aunt, Mrs. Lloyd, in which he not only declares his decision, but also discloses the spirit which animated him in his choice of a profession, he writes to his sister as follows—" My profession has long been chosen in my own mind —long ere I disclosed it to any one. I think the ministry was the very first occupation for life that came into my mind and none other. I can truly say, that nothing has appeared to be compared with it: indeed this thought of serving in the temple of the Lord has afforded me the greatest joy I have experienced. The Lord has been peculiarly gracious unto me through all my rebellings against His Holy Spirit! He has gently led me through the Wilderness to see a faint light of what Heaven is.

"Oh! may He go on and perform His good work begun in me. Use me, good Lord, as seemeth to Thee good, rather than not do work in Thy vineyard let me labor in the meanest corner of it, even in the briars and the thorns where no good seed has ever taken root, and such has been my feelings and I think my heart does not deceive me when I say I am ready to go and preach the Gospel in the most remote and heathen portion of the earth's wide surface; should the Lord see fit to send me. One thing I trust I have not presumed in, namely, that He has called me to serve in His church.

"I feel as well assured of it as though a voice from heaven called me to the work.

## Early Life

"I am further grateful to say, that I can thank not only yourself for the kindness done me, but God who has inclined you to benefit me so greatly. And he adds, "On Sunday we witness the ordination of Charles at this place." How much I wish you could be present. It will be a scene of the deepest joy to our dear parents."

James Lloyd was ever silent and constrained about himself but this letter opens up the soul that was in him, and discloses the intensity of his feelings as regards the sacred ministry.

If he should be able to attain the high calling in Christ Jesus, he would be willing to work with joy in the most barren fields and at the ends of the earth, if called to such a place. Is it a wonder then, that when the voice of the great Missionary Bishop sounded in his ear, his devoted spirit responded, "Here am I, send me!"

His brother Charles Breck became a missionary in northern Pennsylvania, and at first it was planned that James Lloyd should join him in that field. But the appearance of Bishop Kemper, urging the claims of the vast wilderness of the northwest, captured the imagination of this young devotee, and he forthwith gave himself soul and body to the enterprise.

It is related of the two brothers, Charles and James Lloyd, that they read in their vacation, Kip's "Double Witness of the Church," together, looking up and comparing all the references in their Bibles. To get at the root of the matter was ever a characteristic of this intense spirit, and when once convinced of the truth, of his position to dismiss forever all doubt or question respecting its reliability. It is a tradition of him, that he had read, "Foster on the Will," and that it so impressed him that it influenced him through all his life. But for this story we have no authority beyond a common rumor, although it indicates the reputation he had for getting his own way in most things he set out to accomplish.

While at the seminary, James Lloyd attended the "Church of the Holy Communion," of which the Rev. Dr. Mulenberg was rector. Here he taught in the Sunday-school, and was noted for his industry and reliability.

## CHAPTER II

### WISCONSIN

THE difficulty of securing a priest of suitable age and experience to take the headship of the Associate Mission it was proposed to inaugurate in Wisconsin, was finally settled by Bishop Kemper himself. After an interview with the Rev. Mr. Cadle, chaplain at Ft. Crawford, Wisconsin, who was then in the East, he was persuaded to take the position for one year; and so it was arranged that he should meet the young men, Breck, Adams and Hobart at Buffalo, and that they should sail around the lakes to Milwaukee, together. Some rough weather was encountered on Lake Ontario and Lake Huron, but with this exception the journey was without incident and they finally landed on the shores of the new territory, at Milwaukee, where they were met by the good Bishop Kemper, and entertained by him for a season.

Shortly after reaching Milwaukee one of their number, Hobart, started on an exploring expedition to a place called Prairieville, now Wauskeka, twelve miles out from the city. The second Sunday after landing, Mr. Breck had an appointment for services at Elkhorn, forty miles out, where he found a family by the name of Brainerd, of which he gives quite a long account, and as these people were afterwards connected with my own family by marriage, I here take the liberty of repeating the incident in the language of Mr. Breck himself:

"Friday night being Christmas eve, we had services in the schoolhouse, and it was well filled with the settlers of the wilderness. In the afternoon of Christmas day I baptized Mr. Brainerd and nine children of his family. Could you have witnessed this scene your heart would have rejoiced. No church, no altar, no chancel. We assembled in this plain western schoolhouse, which had in its centre a long table that served as our altar. Around this we stood in order, as follows: myself at the back of it, having it before me, and placed on it a rude vessel, serving as a font. The father stood opposite me on the other side, with two adult children on the one side and a third on the other. The witnesses of these were the grandfather and his daughter, Mrs. Brainerd, both communicants. The grandmother was too infirm to stand. She was confirmed by Bishop Seabury. At either end of this long table stood the younger children, four sons at one end and a son and daughter at the other. We occupied the centre of the schoolroom, while the congregation sat all around us with fixed attention, when all were duly baptized. How powerfully did this whole scene strike me as resembling, in some of its features, the accounts contained in the Acts of the Apostles and in the Epistles. 'Stephanas and his household' were baptized there—Brainerd and his household were baptized here."

From statistics furnished to the Domestic Committee, from the first of October to the first of January they had walked 786 miles, and ridden 1,851 miles on horseback, which is at the rate of 10,000 miles a year. They had one student at this time. Prior Cadle had nearly perished from cold, having lost his way on his return from Green Bay. He seemed never to have really identified himself with the mission or its work, and so his loss was little felt when he resigned his position as head of the mission in the spring of 1842. This year found the mission located on the Nashotah Lakes, a choice and beautiful spot, for an institution of its kind. This year, also, witnessed the ordination to the priesthood of Breck and Adams by Bishop Kemper, at Oneida Mission, near Green Bay, a hundred and twenty-five miles to the north of Nashotah. It is seldom a deacon has to walk such a distance—250 miles going and returning—for this object, but it was only a moderate journey for Breck and Adams after they had become accustomed to similar tramps every week to fill their missionary appointments.

This year Mr. Breck was elected by Hobart and Adams to the Deanship of the mission to his great surprise and wonderment, as evidenced by a letter to his sister written at this time. This year was noted for the return of Hobart to the East for reasons which I have never had explained, but which were doubtless satisfactory to himself. Perhaps he was not pleased with the disciplinary side of the Institution, which applied to all from the Dean down to the youngest soul of the brotherhood. A log house of considerable size had been erected near the future site of the seminary. I say considerable size, because it must have been such to house seventeen persons in all, as we are informed it did. I have always thought it remarkable that so many young men could have been gathered together in so short a time. They came from the neighborhood and from distant points as well. Some were picked up by the missionaries as they traveled and others came from the East and South. It was an incongruous gathering of every class and kind and age and grade of men and boys out of which the master made his bricks for the building of his "Religious House," for that was the idea which Mr. Breck had in mind even at this early day, and it was this ambition of his that after the experience of a year or two, disgusted and drove Mr. Adams to resign and return to the East, thus leaving Mr. Breck absolutely alone in the wilderness, with some fourteen mission stations on his hands, and no one to counsel with but the good and wise Bishop Kemper. The that early day, but it took the fancy of these young deacons, and for several years, first at Nashotah and then at St. Paul, Dr. Breck did his best to carry it into effect. As self-denial is the corner-stone of the monastic idea, perhaps it was this that enabled Mr. Breck to achieve a success which, under other conditions and with other motives, might have been impossible.

The articles of the Associate Mission required a celibate clergy and a religious garb of coarse or plain material. Within a year after the arrival of the three young deacons at Prairieville, Wisconsin, one of them, Mr. Hobart, decided to quit the field and return to New York, thus reducing the force by one-third, and leaving Dr. Breck and Adams to solve the problem of work and support by themselves. It seems to have been an essential part of the Associate Mission that there should be at once started a school of the prophets, to educate and prepare men who were on the ground for the work of the Church in the rapidly growing West. In speaking thus far of the Associate Mission, I would not seem to overlook the work of Bishop Kemper, for it was chiefly to this noble and saintly man that Nashotah owed its first impulse. The Rev. Jackson Kemper was consecrated as Bishop of the Northwest and parts adjacent in 1835, and at once set out to visit and explore his rather undefined jurisdiction. To this end he traveled over Wisconsin, Indiana, Illinois, Missouri, and down the

Mississippi to the Gulf, and then through the Southern States, and back again to Wisconsin. After five years' absence, Bishop Kemper returned to New York, and told his story in the ears of the young men who were ready to be ordained to the work of the ministry. This, in a word, was how it came about that the souls of one and another of these young students became enthused for the great enterprise they were about to engage in.

Bishop Kemper was a gentleman of the old school, dignified, courteous, scrupulous in his attire, and exacting in the respect due to his office and himself. This was the character of the man who spent eleven months of each year riding in stage coaches and steamers over his illimitable diocese of the northwest. One month in the year he took as a vacation and remained at home to get even with his correspondence and straighten up his household affairs. It is quite remarkable that in all his travels by stage and steamer, about 4,000 miles a year, he never met with an accident, but on his first journey by rail, he had the misfortune to break an arm.

Shortly after the mission had been located at Nashotah, Bishop Kemper took up his residence near by, in a modest frame house, and there remained until his death, in 1870. The Bishop's family consisted at that time of himself, two maiden sisters, and one daughter, Mrs. Wm. Adams, and his two sons, Samuel and Lewis.

The latter afterwards became a professor at Nashotah, and died, lamented by all who knew him, in 1886. It will be readily seen from his long absences from home that the Bishop could not interest himself practically in Nashotah's affairs, so that from the very first the chief responsibilities of the mission and school fell upon the shoulders of Dr. Breck. Of course, in this statement I do not overlook the staunch support which Dr. Breck received from his fellow-worker, Dr. William Adams, honored in his retirement from active work, and greatly beloved in his old age. (Since this was written Dr. Adams has died.) Both Breck and Adams were equally qualified for the work which God had given them to do, and each in his work was the complement of the other. Dr. Breck was enthusiastic, enterprising, aggressive, and ready to take advantage of opportunities. He was also the financial head of the institution. Dr. Adams was essentially a student and a professor, a man better capable than any one I have known of impressing upon younger minds his own character and stamp of Churchmanship. The Church owes an immeasurable debt to such men as Seabury, White, Hobart, De Lancy, Kip, Otey, Doane, Odenheimer, and Kemper, but to none more than to William Adams, D. D., of Nashotah, for the most wholesome, consistent, and best tempered Churchmanship now prevailing in the American Catholic Church.

When first I knew Nashotah, in 1847, there were thirty-four students resident in the institution; twelve of these were in the theological department. In the preparatory course there were boys of thirteen and men of thirty years of age. Some were from the immediate neighborhood, others from the East and South. From New York City there were two nephews of Dr. Frank Vinton, also James Henry Williams, James Rogers, Edmond D. Cooper, William Jarvis, etc. This will indicate the reputation which Nashotah enjoyed in those early days. Prior to 1847, all the labor was performed by the students. Nashotah at this time was rich in its four hundred and sixty acres of real estate, but as only a small portion was under cultivation, it yielded but a little part of the support for such a large and expensive family. At one time the students did four hours' work in term time and eight hours' in vacation. There was no call for athletics and gymnasiums in those days at Nashotah, but the students excelled in swimming and skating. The culinary department passed away with the eight hours of vacation labor, but the washing committee remained until 1850, when it, too, disappeared with the advent of Dr. Cole as president, succeeding Dr. Breck. The students, however, continued the four hours' work in term time until the new order of things under Dr. Cole, when two hours' only were required. The labor doubtless was a part of the monastic idea, and belonged to the disciplinary side of the institution, although it was really a necessity at first to help out the straightened income. There was no Woman's Auxiliary in those days, yet friends in the East supplied many boxes of clothing every year, the money value of which must have been up in the thousands.

The washing committee was certainly a great saving to Nashotah, probably not less than $10 a week or about $500 a year. This estimate would be the minimum, and perhaps equal to the money value of all the other work done by the students on the four hour, or term-time basis. I should suppose the expenses of Nashotah could not have been less than from ten to twelve thousand dollars a year at that period of its history. To provide this large income was the work to which Dr. Breck diligently applied himself. As there is no effect without an adequate cause, we must find the cause in the pen of the president. With this mighty wand he smote the rock, and the waters flowed in a steady and continuous stream. The daily mail brought many letters, and the larger number contained the offerings of churches and Sunday-schools, and of individual men and women whose hearts were moved with earnest sympathy for this great venture of faith, and for the man who, to them, was its interesting representative. The occasion and the man were both unique. There had been nothing like such a mission in the history of the American Church before; all eyes were centred upon it; all hearts were responsive to its appeals for assistance; and most singular of all was the fact that even when Dr. Breck left Nashotah for St. Paul, in 1850, although the same interest followed him to his new mission, still Nashotah's friends did not desert her, as some feared they might do, and even to this day the "barrel of meal has not wasted, nor the cruse of oil failed" to supply that school of the prophets "with food convenient for them."

## CHAPTER IV

### NASHOTAH—CONTINUED

The early days at Nashotah are of interest because they throw light upon the first work of Dr. Breck, and so assist us to get a better insight into the character of this remarkable man. They are interesting, also, as revealing an order of institutional life, which, it is quite safe to say, will never be repeated in the history of the American Church.

What are known as the early days of Nashotah cover the time from 1842 to March, 1850, a period of eight years. My own acquaintance with Nashotah dates from 1847. In the summer of that year my family moved to Wisconsin and settled within one mile of the institution. That year, also, I first attended the service of the Episcopal Church, held in Nashotah chapel, and wondered at its, to me, strange character. I confess to a frightful ignorance, as I thought they chanted because they did not know how to sing tunes, although I must have been disabused of that idea before the service ended. Altogether I was not pleased with a service where all the prayers were read out of a book. Soon after this, Dr. Breck, then a young man about twenty-seven years of age, called at our house. All I remember of the visit was that he seemed an unusually tall man who sat up very straight on the front of the chair. Soon after this visit I began my preparation for Holy Baptism, going to Dr. Breck's study for recitations of the catechism once a week.

During this time I was given several books to read, besides forms of self-examination and private devotion—Kip's "Double Witness of the Church" I read through twice with great satisfaction. After three months of study, Dr. Breck deemed me ready for the sacred rite, and on a Sunday following, at the afternoon service, I, with fifteen others, was baptized. At the close of the second lesson, all being in white robes, we marched from the chapel down to the lake, and upon the platform of the baptistery, from which six steps led into the water, the candidates were baptized, some kneeling on the steps, when water was poured on their heads from a silver ewer, and others went into the water and were immersed, kneeling and bowing under the water, as is the custom in our Church. Then we returned to the chapel, and the service went on to its conclusion. I recall that the font, which stood by the door of the chapel, was so large that infants were often immersed. On one occasion the ice was cut in the lake and two young ladies were submerged in the chilly waters. All this was in the line of Dr. Breck's idea that

Christians should learn to "endure hardness as good soldiers of Jesus Christ."

By this circumstance I am reminded of an incident in the early life of Nashotah, and before my day, when a summer outing was projected for the students to Green Bay, Wis., where our Church had a mission among the Oneida Indians, the real object of this journey being the ordination of Messrs. Breck and Adams to the priesthood, Bishop Kemper having arranged to meet them there. In the way of hardening the seventeen students, Dr. Breck determined to call the 6 o'clock A. M. roll on the pier which extended into the lake some forty feet, and on the end of which was a long spring-board. As the names were called the young men were expected to answer, and casting each his garment away, one after another to plunge into the water. This was considered to be the right sort of discipline and hardening for the six weeks of camp life before them. Canute Peterson, a Swede of eighteen years of age, who was one of the expedition, penned some verses on one occasion, of which I recall but two lines, but they are very suggestive of other things that might have happened in those night encampments. "Of a morning surprise," he says, "we were as wet as we could be, and Halstead's calf ate up our tea."

When first I saw Nashotah, there was nothing attractive about it but its situation. Dr. Breck had an artistic eye for locating his missions and schools. The twin lakes (Nashotah) were ideal in their beauty and surroundings. From the plateau one could catch a glimpse of three lakes beside the one on which the mission was located and from a high elevation three miles distant, fifteen lakes are visible, but none have the quiet and serene beauty of the Nashotah Lakes. In 1848 when I entered the institution, there were thirty-four students, of whom twelve were candidates for orders, and the remainder were in the collegiate department, their ages ranging from fourteen upwards to thirty years. These students lived in thirty-four rooms. Every student must have his own room. Four were under the chapel, eight in St. Lazarus row, two in the ice-house, one in the wash-house, four in the blue house, where Dr. Breck was domiciled. It would be difficult to say where the rest found quarters.

A day at Nashotah began at 5 o'clock A. M., with the ringing of a bell which hung thirty feet up in a tree, near the blue house, and the bell was always rung by Dr. Breck himself. Five minutes after this, the second peal summoned every student to answer to his name, which was called at the door of a small central building that served as a library. With a scramble into trousers and shoes, and a blanket or quilt thrown about him, the student rushed out to within hearing and answering distance, and then returned shivering to his room to make his fire, to dress and study until six o'clock, when the bell rang again. This time the young men ranged themselves in line in front of headquarters, answered again to their names, and marched to chapel, where the whole Morning Prayer was said. At 6:30 we had breakfast, when a good cup or bowl of coffee revived our drooping spirits. From seven to nine o'clock there was study in our rooms, and then began the recitations of the day. At 12:30 there was dinner, and at 1 P. M. work began and continued until five o'clock. Then at six o'clock we again assembled in front of the blue house to answer to our names, and attend chapel and then to supper, and after that we went to our rooms for study until 10 P. M., when lights were out for the night, but on occasion they were re-lit and a few chosen spirits enjoyed the forbidden smoke. I think the only thing in the way of hazing in those days was to invite the newcomer who did not smoke, and then lock the door and smudge him. On one occasion I recall, Dr. Breck appeared, but was unable to enter as the dense cloud forbade him, and he, not being a smoker himself, beat a hasty retreat, but not until he had "spotted" a few of the transgressors. There was nothing a student so much dreaded as a summons to headquarters for an interview with the president. It always meant business. From this instance it is easy to see that Dr. Breck was the present as well as the presiding, genius of Nashotah. His personal oversight extended to every detail; nothing escaped his scrupulous attention. He would have been a martinet in the army. Dr. Breck, however, failed to perceive that arbitrary discipline could be carried too far. He did not know that boys grew to be men even at college. He had one rule for the boy of fourteen and the man of thirty years, and this led to rebellion, and was one reason for his resignation of the presidency.

Dr. Breck did not, however, yield gracefully when he had made a mistake; he could not retreat. He could lead, but not follow, and the results were what might have been expected. In every case he was judge, jury and executioner. No one could say when his own case would be called. It was reasonably certain among the younger men that there was a growing case against them, even if they were not conscious of wrong-doing. It was only a question of time when the cloud would burst, when the dreaded summons to an interview with the president in his study would be received. This condition reached a climax in 1859, when Samuel Josiah Hayward was expelled for insubordination. Mr. Hayward said he would not be treated like a boy of fifteen, and the president answered by expelling him. It was a serious matter for Mr. Hayward, but it had an amusing side also. The question of expulsion was a matter for the faculty to act upon, and as that body was small, two members constituted a quorum. As I heard the story, Dr. Breck was chairman, and Dr. Adams, the other mem-

## Nashotah—Continued

ber, present. The case was stated by the president, but on the question of expulsion, Dr. Adams voted no, Dr. Breck, aye; then the president claimed his privilege of casting the deciding vote in case of a tie, which settled the matter, and the culprit was judicially dismissed. But the end was not yet. When the time arrived for Josiah to get his small, round-top hair trunk down to the stage road, a third of a mile away, the order came to the assembled students, that no one should countenance the disgraced man by assisting him to get his baggage off. This was a serious matter for the outgoing student, as there was nothing but hand power to rely on, not even a wheelbarrow being available.

This order was the "last straw." The young men rushed to see which could get hold of the trunk handles first. It was indeed a triumphal procession, and before the trunk was on the stage, all the boys in turn had hold of the handles to carry it. Of course, no one was punished for this multitudinous offense. It was shortly after this that Dr. Breck resigned the presidency, and came East to prepare for his mission to St. Paul, Minn.

*A very good story but the dates at least must be wrong. S.J.N. graduated at N. in 1855 & was ord. deacon & priest in same year.*

*1859 obviously misprint for 1849.*

## CHAPTER V

### NASHOTAH—IN 1847

THERE were no snap shots or photograph fiends in the early days of Nashotah, and it is only by a kindly providence that a sketch, made by one of the students, Eugene C. Pattison, was preserved.

It is an excellent representation of old Nashotah in the last days of Dr. Breck's presidency, 1849. We are looking from the lake side, and thus secure the water-front view, which every alumnus will recognize, especially men of the fifties and sixties.

Beginning on the left, at the water's edge, we have the wash-house and laundry, very indistinct; next, the ice-house, then on the hill the blue house, so named from its color. This was headquarters where the young men lined up for the march to chapel, morning and evening, at six o'clock. Next, and to the right a little, is the kitchen and dining-room, then the storehouse, and beyond, still, was a long building of one story containing eight single rooms, four on either side, each opening onto a porch which protected the entrance from storms. This was really the **aristocratic** part of the institution,

GEN. THEO. SEMINARY
LIBRARY
NEW YORK

NASHOTAH IN 1847.

where the seniors and a favored, pampered few found shelter, and was most appropriately named "St. Lazarus' Row"; and, come to think of it, I suppose this poor saint must have been Nashotah's patron saint in all those days of struggle when every man paid for his privileges by the sweat of his brow.

In the centre of the picture, we have a small frame building, known then as the library, from the door of which, in the bleak winter mornings at five o'clock, Dr. Breck, with a lantern under his arm, called the roll, a very trying ordeal for young fellows who were enjoying the best nap of the night; but I seldom heard any complaint "that thus it must be." There were other small buildings where students were housed, as the carpenter shop and the henhouse, so called, while four found shelter under the chapel, the building on the right and directly in our front.

As I recall it, these seem indeed the happiest, if they were among the hardest, days of Nashotah's history. Common trials develop brotherly feeling. Except that our quarters were small, we were well off. We had always a comfortable table under Dr. Breck's administration, and the storeroom was well supplied by friends in the East with warm clothing, even if the fit of things was not always to the form of the wearer.

One cannot form a correct idea of those days at Nashotah without taking into consideration the fact that Nashotah chapel was the parish

church of St. Sylvanus parish. The president of
Nashotah House was rector of this parish, which
had an important constituency outside the institution in the surrounding country. The following names of families will be readily recalled by
the alumni of those days: There were Mr. and
Mrs. Slingerland and their daughter, Hettie, who
became the wife of the Rev. N. Rue High; there
were the Douglases, the Barnards, the Jessups,
the Guerneses, the Castlemans, the Seymours, the
Frisbys, and the family of the Bishop; and last,
but not least in importance, was the large household of Samuel Breck, the brother of the president. It was, in fact, quite an aristocratic congregation, for all these were what might be called
gentlemen farmers or men of the legal or medical
profession. In those times it is evident that each
Sunday was a high day for the students. Some
of these families were exceedingly hospitable,
and Saturday, between one and six o'clock, being
a half holiday, excellent use was made of it in
calling on these friends and neighbors who lived
anywhere from two to five miles distant.

At first, and for several years, Mr. Samuel
Breck's home was a comfortable house at the
head of the lake, half a mile away. This family
consisted of Mr. Breck and wife and six children,
beside the housekeeper who came with them
from the East. Five of these children were
daughters, and three of them of a very interesting age; although at that time quite young, yet

they were dainty flowers, and gave promise of a grace and beauty, which after years fully justified. The entrance of this family at the chapel on Sunday morning was always attended with something of a sensation. One, the third daughter, was very fair and rather delicate, and had a way of fainting now and then in the services from long kneeling and the close air, and then her father and one of the older students would remove her to a convenient room until she recovered. Only once were my poor quarters favored with her presence, being very conveniently situated under the chapel itself. It may seem a trifling circumstance to the reader, but had he lived in those days, and stood in my shoes, he would not be skeptical of the effect produced by such an incident in the life of a modest Nashotah student, who could only admire and worship such divinities from afar.

It can well be imagined that Sunday was a veritable oasis in the desert of our social life, and especially of female society. I may add that but one of these young ladies became the wife of a clergyman. Mary Breck, the eldest daughter, married the Rev. Peter Brown Morrison—whose twin brother so strongly resembled him that even Mrs. Breck hardly knew them apart.

There was no such vexing question then, as now, about "Labor and Capital." Then it was only labor, and hard labor at that, for men professing to lead the life of students. I have heard it said that labor is dignified or degraded by the spirit of the laborer. I certainly have always been proud of my part in assisting to lay foundations in the West, and very grateful for the experience gained at Nashotah.

In the earlier days at Nashotah they turned their hand to any service. They farmed and gardened. They wrought in the kitchen and wash-house. They chopped down great oaks in the forest, and sawed and split them fine for fuel, and whatsoever "their hand found to do they did it with their might." There was no football then, nor baseball, nor any sort of gymnasium for athletic exercises, and none were needed. A stern necessity compelled them to do their own work, and in this they wrought diligently and "endured hardness as good soldiers of Jesus Christ."

# CHAPTER VI

## DIVERSITIES OF LABOR

OF all the diversities of labor at Nashotah in those primitive times, perhaps the washing or laundry committee attracted most attention and excited the chiefest comment. This part of the work was perhaps least desirable in the estimation of some, and yet it was most exclusive, being composed of selected men. For several years the Rev. John O. Barton, D. D., was the head of this department. His room adjoined the washhouse, and he had the right to choose his assistants. He tolerated no indifferent material. I recall no name that was not that of a man who possessed habits of personal neatness and good taste in his apparel. There was on this committee at various times a nephew of Dr. Frank Vinton, a grandson of Bishop Jarvis, an archdeacon, the Rev. Henry C. Shaw, and the writer of the present history. It was, in a sense, the aristocratic committee of its day. It enjoyed peculiar favors and exemptions. Even the president could hardly venture a word of criticism. On Monday, coffee was served with the lunch, an unusual concession. Each student was allowed twelve pieces a week, and brought his own pillowslip of soiled linen bright and early Monday morning, often throwing it to the bottom of the hill, or using it for a toboggan on the icy track in winter. There were always between four and five hundred pieces in the wash, including the kitchen and dining-room contingent, a herculean task, but the wash was usually on the line by five o'clock in the afternoon of Monday. Tuesday was a holiday for this committee, nothing further being done until Wednesday, when a beginning was made in the ironing. Thursday and Friday afternoons completed the task, and each one of the committee on Saturday night was credited duly with his twenty-two hours for the week. The comment of our Sunday visitors was that "the linen of the students was exceptionally white and well laundried."

It was the experience gained in this school of the prophets which enabled the writer to save a great many dollars to the mission at St. Paul, in 1850–2. In those days men worked their way into the ministry, and only such as would and could work, attained the prize of that "high calling in Christ Jesus." At this period there were thirty-four students at Nashotah, of whom twelve were in the theological department. There was also a good parish school kept in Nashotah's first brick building.

The Rev. Mr. Markoe I remember to have heard preach in this place, and I also heard him

## Diversities of Labor

read the Old Testament lesson about Sisera and Jael in such a way as to make my hair rise, and my knees to tremble. I recall the lesson but not the sermon. Like Dr. Berkley, of St. Louis, Markoe was no advocate of "colorless reading," which so many affect in these days of insipidity in rendering our noble liturgy and reading to the people the Word of the living God. Yes, I remember the lesson, but not the sermon, although Dr. Markoe was a vigorous preacher. This bright but eccentric man became soon after a pervert to Rome. I met him many times afterwards in St. Paul, unfrocked, and a layman. Rome seems to have but little use for a man of intelligence, and somehow soon manages to smother out of him all his ambitions and hopes.

Speaking of Markoe reminds me of a curious fact in the life of Nashotah as a university, in its power of conferring degrees. She has from the first taken a singular position, and here is the anomaly, that she has been as free of her B. D.'s as stingy of her D. D.'s. Her worthy sons go without, or go to others for honor, as if she did not regard her own sons worthy of all honors that should be conferred on them. Dr. Cole, of blessed memory, confessed it to me a mistaken policy in the past, but hoped for better things in the future. "There is that withholdeth more than is meet but it tendeth to poverty."

What Nashotah needs greatly to-day is the further endowment of professorships, and money to complete her new quadrangle so auspiciously begun. Nashotah's past and the memories which cluster round her romantic history should kindle the enthusiasm of noble souls for her future well-being. Already she has sent out over 300 well equipped soldiers, a truly noble showing, fully justifying the wisdom and prescience of him whom the noble Archbishop of Canterbury named "The Apostle of the Wilderness," James Lloyd Breck; and that other name, than which none is more worthy of honor, William Adams, who lived long to rejoice in the noble work God graciously gave him to do in educating the faithful ministers who in almost every land to-day proclaim the unchanging faith of the Church of Jesus Christ.

## CHAPTER VII

### A RELIGIOUS HOUSE

In a history of Dr. Breck and the work at Nashotah it is important that we note some of the trials and difficulties which befel him after he had been chosen Dean of the seminary, and the efforts he made to establish a "Religious House."

It was partly in consequence of this effort that Hobart left him and returned East, and that Mr. Adams deserted him later and only came back when he was assured that he could live outside the institution, and that he should be foot-loose and free to do as he pleased. This "Religious House" idea or plan of Mr. Breck's was in no sense a Romish idea as some outsiders intimated. Some were glad of an opportunity to bring "a railing accusation" against any one of a Catholic mind, who bowed in the creed, or honored the cross, or celebrated the Holy Communion oftener than once a month. "Dr. Breck's plan" included a "Celibate Clergy and a Lay Brotherhood," all of which he believed might exist in the Church. He always fought the idea that Rome was specially entitled to all the good things, and he believed that the best way to oppose her was by showing that it was not necessary to go out of the Church to organize a "Religious House" or a Brotherhood, if such things were desirable in the American Catholic Church to which he belonged ; but I am constrained to say that Dr. Breck was alone in his idea. There was not a clergyman or a student connected with Nashotah at that time who believed in or sympathized with the idea, and consequently he was left alone for a considerable period. Adams and Hobart left him with eight missions on his hands, and he the only clergyman to supply them. There was then trouble and perplexity until Mr. Adams returned to relieve the straitened situation; then also the Lay Brotherhood was formed and through their assistance the work of clergymen was partially supplied. "When the worst comes, then things begin to mend." Dr. Breck soon discovered that his plan for a "Religious House" would not work, and gave up (at Bishop Kemper's suggestion) the idea as impractical. He confessed to the Bishop that he had made a mistake and that it must be attributed to the inexperience of his youth, but it was a hard and bitter pill to swallow, for a man of his unbending will. When I went to Nashotah in September, 1848, I knew nothing of the past of Nashotah's experience, but I did hear that a certain young lady had been sent east for a year, and that Mr. Adams' going and returning had been in some way connected with this circumstance and some said that Mr. Adams' stipulation that he should not live in the institution, was connected with his intention to marry the young lady who had been won by his devotion and faithfulness.

While I was at Nashotah one and a half years at that time, several parties visited us from a distance. Dr. Shelton and another, whose name I do not recall. The Rev. Brothers Clapp and Haskins of New York City wandered our way, and were much entertained by the primitive look of things; Dr. Shelton we called the "Buffalo" because of his personal appearance and the place of his residence. He was a kindly man with a big voice, and a great curly head, as I remember him. It was some time in 1849 that Rome really invaded Nashotah in the person of the Rev. Gardner Jones. He came from, no one knew where, with letters of introduction but no letter dimissory. He was a large man in mid life, with a full beard and a great voice that added much to the impression which his eloquence made on the students. I recall to-day a sermon in Lent, on "Hell," which frightened us all, and shortly after this the faculty decided that he must leave or show his pedigree and papers. Jones took the hint and French leave also. The last seen of him he stood alone on the bank of the lake looking over the grounds. Afterwards he was traced to various places, but finally he turned up at "Notre Dame," Indiana, a Romish Seminary, and so proved himself to be a Jesuit in disguise. Dr.

Breck's name was never connected with this incident, but to my thinking Jones had heard that there was trouble inside the walls and had come to see for himself whether there was not a chance for the wolf to carry off a sheep or two for his own delectation. Indeed it was not long after this that Rev. Markoe and his whole family dropped into the enemies' camp, much as the Lambert family did afterwards in St. Paul. It is surprising how active the Jesuits were in those early days, and how successful they were in making proselytes to Rome. But, however high Dr. Breck's ideas were for those days, he had no use for Rome or her monstrous claims. Of this I am confident, from the way he treated Romanizers in St. Paul, and afterwards at the Indian Mission. When Dr. Breck resigned the Presidency of Nashotah house there was a mortgage on the property of $1,200 and interest. The money was borrowed of the Rev. Mr. Davis at Green Bay, but rather than have the institution in debt, Dr. Breck sacrificed his own last property, an inheritance from a relative, and sent the money in gold by the hand of his private secretary, the Rev. George P. Schetkoy, who carried it in a belt about his waist, over one hundred miles, on foot, to deliver it safely to Mr. Davis; so that Dr. Breck could say in leaving, "I owe no man anything"—nor do I owe one dollar in the world. One day in March, 1850, all the students were called together, thirty-four of them, and were informed that all could pack their trunks and scatter each to his own place. It was thunder out of a clear sky. Personally I had not far to go, but others went south and east to their distant homes, all except twelve theological students who remained to complete their course. On Dr. Breck's nomination the Rev. Azel D. Cole, a classmate of his at the Seminary, was elected to the Presidency. Dr. Breck soon returned to the East to prepare for his new mission to St. Paul, a place and territory of which I had never heard, five hundred miles to the northwest and near the Arctic Circle, as it seemed to me.

## CHAPTER VIII

### JAMES LLOYD BRECK

BEFORE starting on the journey to St. Paul, perhaps it may be well to say something further of Dr. Breck's personality.

If "the study of mankind is man," then it would be inexcusable not to get better acquainted with our hero as an individual. As Dr. Breck's work was of an extraordinary kind, so was the man himself unique in his personality. On the street or in the house, anywhere and at all times, he attracted attention and commanded respect. Like Saul, the king, he was head and shoulders above his fellows. He stood six feet four inches, and appeared even taller than that, by reason of his erect and almost military bearing. He impressed one always as an officer on duty. His dress was in its way a uniform, and of the best material. His clerical coat reached to his knees, and was closely buttoned from the throat down to the waist. His linen was of the finest, and always scrupulously clean. In a word, Dr. Breck was one of the best dressed clergymen I have ever met; and this neatness of attire belonged to the style of the man. His hair was light in color and thin, and his eyes were blue and soft. Dr.

Breck was well born and well bred, and if "manners make the man" then he had been a man, without other qualifications. It was noticeable that he never made any use of the back of a chair, but sat straight on the very edge, and his hat was off always where there was a roof over him, or in his hand when advancing to meet distinguished visitors, long before he grasped their hands in friendly greeting. Physically, Dr. Breck always seemed to be in perfect health, and he certainly exhibited wonderful endurance. He rose at five o'clock and retired at ten. I do not remember to have seen him sleeping in the day time, nor did I ever hear him say that he was tired or hungry. That he was no idler, goes without saying. He certainly possessed the very genius of industry. I never knew him to miss the smallest opportunity on stage or steamer or in hotel for writing letters and getting them off at once. These white-winged messengers "flew as doves to their windows," and returned laden with the dew of God's blessing, for all of them were sped on the wings of prayer. Essentially this great missionary was a believer in "a God who heareth prayer." I never knew him on any occasion to omit his stated devotions. He made no parade of his piety, nor did he shrink from publicity when it was unavoidable.

James Lloyd Breck was born near Bristol, Pa., in 1820, and was therefore in 1842 just twenty-two years of age. He was twenty-seven when I first knew him, and even at that time he did not impress me as a young man. He was indeed a youth in years and experience; some of the students were older than the president at that period of his history. Much could have been overlooked in the mistakes of so inexperienced a person, if any were ever made.

This grave, but very young, president of Nashotah House was not altogether without capacity for a little relaxation along the lines of youthful sports. I recall several occasions when there had been a considerable snowfall, he would join the younger boys in a snow-balling bout, to their intense delight. These frolics were always after dark. As he ran like a deer, it was difficult to catch him, even when all were in opposition, and when at last, exhausted, he went down in the struggle, and was rolled over and over in the snow, he always took his punishment with the best possible grace.

I think it can be said with truth that Dr. Breck was fond of children. He always enjoyed catechising them, and would have them stand in front of him in a semicircle, while he sat on the elevation of the choir steps. Where he got the idea I do not know, but generally he had a large, black bag with him, and at the end of the catechising he would thrust his hand down into its mysterious depths and bring to the surface all manner of cards and surprises, which he proceeded to distribute to the wide-eyed youngsters as rewards for regular attendance or good recitations. That bag was a mystery and hence a power.

Dr. Breck was very particular about giving Baptismal and Confirmation certificates and Prayer Books to those who were baptized or confirmed. I cherished mine for years. I think he was wise in giving attention to these details, and that he realized in his own day what others are beginning to appreciate now, that the Book of Common Prayer can speak for itself, and that it is the best missionary tract in the world.

The debt which the Church owes to Dr. Breck is a large one. He, beyond all our missionaries, illustrated the life of faith in the world. He believed that he was doing God's work, and that He would sustain him. It was this sublime conviction which sent him forth into the wilderness. All the great missionaries of the Church, from St. Paul down to this day, have possessed a similar faith and a like enthusiasm. He never for one moment doubted that the daily mail would bring the daily bread, and when he left Nashotah to establish a new associate mission at St. Paul, he went forth with only a small sum of ready money in his possession, but in a spirit of exalted faith that he would be sustained if he continued faithful. It is given to few men to make such ventures for Christ in the missionary field. Dr. Breck, in a statesman-like spirit, grasped the situation at once that the West must educate and send forth her own clergy. Almost from the beginning there were postulants for the ministry gathered in from families visited in the first missionary excursions.

At a very early day, also, Dr. Breck purchased 465 acres of land at the government price of $1.25 an acre, and this remains to-day, the property of Nashotah. The same kind of an investment of a few hundred dollars was made by him in St. Paul for Church purposes, and what is left of that seven acres located in the centre of the city, is now valued at over $100,000.

In all this that is written of Dr. Breck I do not desire to be thought blind to his weaknesses or his faults. "No man is a hero to his page," and I knew him intimately, in the home, in the Church, and "in journeyings often," and found him ever true to his purposes. It was my fortune to enter Minnesota with him in 1850, and sixteen years later, when he left for California, it so happened that I was the very last person to say good-bye to him on the steamer at Winona. I had seen little of him for some years before that, and the coincidence was so striking that he spoke of it very feelingly, and for the first time in all our intercourse he embraced and kissed me, while the tears coursed down his cheeks, remembering as he did that it was his leave-taking of Minnesota forever.

When the three young deacons left New York in 1841, it was understood that they should live celibate lives for three years at least, but Dr. Breck did not marry for four times three years and more. In the earlier part of Dr. Breck's celibate life he was the ideal knight of the Cross to hundreds of people in the East. The distance, the wildness of the unknown country, the hardships of the life, his extreme youth, the novelty of his itinerating labors, and his striking personality, all appealed to the imagination of Eastern Churchmen, and to Churchwomen especially, and created an enthusiasm for the hero of it all, such as no one at this day can possibly imagine.

It might be said that there was not that intellectual make-up in the man which justified this adulation, as has often been said of Washington and others who achieved great things "under favoring skies" on a modest capital, and yet there are the results to be accounted for! "God seeth not as man seeth." In the shepherd boy He found the king, and in the fishermen of Galilee He discovered the men of His right hand, of whom it was once said in a certain city: "These who have turned the world upside down, are come hither also."

It requires all sorts of people to make a world, and we are apt to belittle qualities we do not possess, and especially such qualities in others as are liable to excess. Some men, we say, are conservative and therefore safe; others are agitators, enthusiasts, idealists, and so dangerous to the settled order of things. James Lloyd Breck

was the apostle of a new era in the Church. He
carried the Church to the very front and planted
her banner on the outposts of the civilization of
his day. He did not wait for railroads or revenues assured. He did not appeal for men from
the East, but raised up men for himself. He did
not rely on others, nor stand on the order of his
going, but went on and on to Nashotah, and St.
Paul, and the Indian mission, beyond the great
river, and then beyond the mountains to the
Pacific Coast.

It is easy now to discern the mistakes of his
youth and inexperience. Easy to say that he
wanted this or that endowment, as an orator, or
a student, or professor, or even as the head of an
educational institution, but then, he was great
in what he stood for—faith, courage, foresight,
convictions, self-reliance, devotion to duty, and a
sublime trust in God. His greatest successes
were achieved at an age when most men are
trying to decide what they will attempt. With
his armor on and lance in rest he rode to the fray
and won his spurs before the Church was aware
that a hero had gone forth to the battle.

There is something greater than a cheap con-
servatism, which is but a name for a timid and
often cowardly spirit, and that is, "achievement." "What hast thou done?" "How much
has thy talent gained?" Measured by God's
standard of fruit, and by achievement, the name
of James Lloyd Breck stands at the head of all

our missionaries, and some day the Church will recognize that in honoring him she is adding yet another star to the jewels of her crown.

And this word, star, recalls an incident with which I close this personal sketch of Dr. Breck. One evening shortly after I went to Nashotah as a student, I was standing by his side, in the open, when he said, pointing to the spangled heavens: "I always think on such a night as this, when the stars are shining so brilliantly, how encouraging to the ministers of Jesus Christ is the Scripture which reads: 'They that will be wise shall shine as the brightness of the firmament, and they that turn many to righteousness as the stars forever and ever.'"

## CHAPTER IX

### THE JOURNEY TO ST. PAUL

EARLY in June, 1850, Dr. Breck returned from the East, accompanied by two clergymen, the Rev. Timothy Wilcoxson and the Rev. John A. Merrick, a deacon just in orders. These clergymen, with Dr. Breck, remained a week at Nashotah recuperating from the long and tedious journey from New York. On Dr. Breck's resignation of the presidency, all the preparatory students left for their several homes. Twelve theological students remained. Meanwhile, the Rev. Azel D. Cole, a classmate of Dr. Breck's, and formerly rector of St. Luke's Church, Racine, had become president of Nashotah House.

I immediately called on Dr. Breck upon his arrival, and begged him to let me go with him to St. Paul, where I understood a new Nashotah was to be started. After considerable hesitation he consented, and so on the 14th of June, 1850, the journey began. It was by stage to Milwaukee and then by railroad, sixty miles, to Janesville, Wis., and then by stage again, 120 miles, to Galena, Ill., where we embarked on the good steamer *Nominee* for St. Paul, 400 miles up the Mississippi. Saturday afternoon found us

## The Journey to St. Paul

up as far as Prairie La Crosse, then a hamlet of three or four houses, where we landed and remained until the following Tuesday, because Dr. Breck would not travel on Sunday. The next day being Sunday, and no place for a service ready, it was determined to go out to the bluff, about a mile distant as it looked, but which we found to be nearer two miles than one. Then a climb to the top of the bluff, 300 feet high, where we held our service, which consisted of Morning Prayer and the Holy Communion. Brother Wilcoxson preached a sermon; the other three, sitting on the rocks around, constituted the congregation. The following day, Monday, no steamer being due before Tuesday, an expedition was organized to cross the river and take possession of Minnesota in the name of Holy Church.

I have often since that time tried, in passing, to locate the place of our landing, and have wondered how these men, totally inexperienced, could have ventured to encounter the strong current of the broad river, especially in a common dugout, or log canoe. As a boy I had experience with this sort of craft and easily managed my small vessel, but the three brethren who took passage together in a large clumsy affair, stemmed the current with difficulty and got over only after a prolonged struggle. I do not believe they quite realized the danger and difficulty of the undertaking. Having fastened our canoes to the bank and found a place suitable for the purpose, Brother Merrick chopped down a small tree, about four inches in diameter, and cutting off a piece five feet long, he bound it with twigs to another tree, into which he had cut a notch about five feet from the ground, thus forming a cross, at the foot of which the Holy Communion was celebrated. The altar was a stone brought from the place of our Sunday service. I was personally much interested in this service, as I was filled with great fear lest Indians might appear out of the dark forests and disturb our devotions and perhaps carry away our scalps as trophies. There was full Morning Prayer and Holy Communion, but no sermon this time. I withdrew from the service at this point and stood at the water's edge with one foot on my canoe and a small pistol in my hand, ready for any emergency. I flattered myself that I was a sentinel on guard, but the service seemed to be interminable, and it was with great thankfulness I echoed the last amen on that occasion.

We returned as we came, having formally taken possession of Minnesota in the name of God and Holy Church. To my boyish mind it seemed a lucky escape from the savages, but to Dr. Breck and the two brethren it was a most real and sacred act of consecration of the soil which they intended to occupy; while to the savages, if ever they saw it, that lone and neglected cross must have been an object of wonder, an outpost of civilization from which its defenders had retreated.

On the afternoon of the Sunday a service was held in the house of a Mr. Levi and the baptism of his infant child was celebrated.

Tuesday afternoon, the 25th of June, we took passage on the stern-wheel steamer *Yankee* for St. Paul, where we arrived in the forenoon of June 27th, 1850. In the afternoon we steamed up to Fort Snelling, four miles, reaching there about sunset. The Rev. E. G. Geer, D. D., then chaplain of the post, was at the wharf to welcome us. I presume to say that our coming was the happiest day of his ministerial life. It was the day he had prayed and waited for; the realization of his dreams for the future of the Church in that new territory.

The missionaries were received with every expression of gladness and a large-hearted hospitality I shall never forget. We were escorted in triumph to his quarters in the fort, and for nearly a week were bountifully entertained. The day following our arrival, our party was driven up to Minnehaha Falls and from there on to St. Anthony Falls, passing over the ground where the beautiful city of Minneapolis now stands, but which, at that time, had not a single house to bless itself withal, or one thing to indicate or prophesy its present greatness. There were in the Territory at that time three important towns: St. Anthony, Stillwater, and St. Paul, the largest,

with about twelve hundred inhabitants. The
first two were settled by lumbermen from Maine.
The population of St. Paul at this time was made
up of three classes: French, half breeds from
Canada, the American Fur Company, and a good
many young men who had come out to seek their
fortunes, mostly single men.

There was on the bluff fronting the river a
Roman Catholic church built of logs; there were
also two small schoolhouses and two hotels of
some pretensions, and in the upper town a Presbyterian church, presided over by E. D. Neil, a
man of intelligence and enterprise, and to whom
St. Paul is much indebted in many ways. Dr.
Geer had visited and held occasional services in
one of the schoolhouses for several years, as he
was able, and it was in this schoolhouse that
services were arranged for by Dr. Breck, on Sunday the 30th of June, 1850.

There were no marked incidents on the voyage
up the river which throw light upon the character of Dr. Breck, except that the regular full
Morning Prayer was said each day in one of our
staterooms, including the "dearly beloved brethren," greatly to my discomfort of mind and body.
A Mississippi steamer stateroom is not a large
affair at the best; about seven feet in length by
six feet in width, one-half of which is occupied
by the berths; three feet by six was therefore
the size of our chapel. The two clergymen, not
including Dr. Breck, who stood at the east end

when he could, sat upon the side of the lower berth, while I, perched on the upper berth, solemnly overlooked the proceedings below. I should have been very well content, only that I was in mortal terror lest there should be listeners who would wonder and smile, perhaps, at our concentrated and almost secret rites. I never could quite understand the motive Dr. Breck had in seeming to be continually on the hunt to find a spreading tree or suitable place for the full Morning Prayer, unless it was that in this way we were spreading the Nashotah idea out over all the northwest, "from the rising of the sun to the going down of the same."

Thirty miles above La Crosse we passed the site of Winona, now a beautiful city of 25,000 inhabitants, then, I remember, a prairie about seven miles long by one in breadth, backed by a rocky bluff, three hundred feet high, and at the centre, on the river bank, the tents of Wabasha and his small band. Forty miles further up we came to the foot of Lake Pepin, a beautiful sheet of water, thirty miles in length and an average of perhaps three miles in width. Four miles above the lake, in a sharp bend of the river, we saw the place which was to be the future city of Red Wing, with its picturesque surroundings; at that time an Indian encampment held quiet possession. Fifteen miles further up we came to the junction of the St. Croix River with the Mississippi. The St. Croix comes in from the north, and appears to be the continuation of the Mississippi, and this appearance is strengthened by the width of the stream, which is really Lake St. Croix, at the upper end of which the city of Stillwater is situated. It is from this place, Point Prescott, that the great river, not so great here, deflects to the northwest for thirty miles, where in going up it strikes a bluff which turns the course of the stream to the southwest; a mile from this turn, on the right and on a level plateau, a hundred feet above the water, stands St. Paul, in a circumvallation of bluffs, which, starting high from the river, like an arm encircle the city. On the west side it passes on up to Fort Snelling, four miles, not touching the river-front within half a mile, until it reaches the fort. In the centre of the circle, in the elbow of the hills, where they dip lowest, half a mile back from the edge of the first bluff, was located the new mission. To the right and left as you faced the south, a commanding view of the upper and lower towns could be obtained. It was upon this vantage ground that I spent many hours of every week watching for the signs of a coming steamer round the bend, for this was our only means of correspondence with the outside world in 1850, and only twice a week did we hear the whistle or catch a sight of the steamer as it appeared far away beyond the intervening forest. About three miles below St. Paul there was a very shallow place known as "Pig's Eye Bar," on which steamers in low water were detained often for twenty-four hours, a very tantalizing thing to business men. It is needless to say that half of the inhabitants of the town turned out to greet every fresh arrival. I remember that there came to live with us from somewhere, a colored boy about eleven years of age who had a very shrill and remarkably piercing voice; he could imitate a steamer's whistle so exactly that it was often mistaken for it, to the discomfiture of many who rushed out expecting a letter by that very boat. He was voted a nuisance, generally, but still he shrieked, to the vexation of the credulous, but to his own intense delight.

## CHAPTER X

### THE ASSOCIATE MISSION IN ST. PAUL

ALTHOUGH there were three clergymen associated in this mission, there was but one ruling spirit. It was he who first promoted the enterprise and assumed all the responsibility of its success. James Lloyd Breck was a man of strong convictions and entirely self-reliant. These qualities were in the man's make-up. He not only believed in God but he also believed in himself. His entire life proved it. The annual expenses of Nashotah must have been from ten to fifteen thousand dollars. The cost of the new mission at St. Paul was less, but whatever that expense was, he assumed it. I was told that the expenses of the first two years of the Indian mission were not far from thirty thousand dollars. How did he raise this money and from whence did his support come? None but those who were of his household could have imagined the extent of his correspondence. In his facile hand the power of the pen was abundantly illustrated. He wrote well and he wrote continually. He wrote letters and articles for the missions, and the object of his writing was to secure funds from churches, Sunday-schools, and individual Church people.

There was something about the man and his ideas that stimulated the missionary spirit as no other man has. Every mail brought remittances. His constant prayer, "Give us this day our daily bread," was daily answered. Was there ever such another instance of sublime faith and splendid achievement in all the history of the American Church? And his monuments, they remain with us to-day in the churches which he planted and in the successful institutions of learning of which he was the founder. His nature was chivalrous. He was a true knight of the Cross. It is said that "no man is a hero to his page." I lived with him, ate and drank with him; I knew his infirmities and his weaknesses, as well as his sterling qualities, and, take him all in all, I verily believe the Church will never look upon his like again. I count it a special providence that it was my good fortune to have known and been admitted by his hands into the Church of Jesus Christ.

Speaking of men, I desire to say, that in the two clergymen which he selected to be with him, the Rev. Timothy Wilcoxson and John Austin Merrick, M. A., deacon, Dr. Breck made no mistake. Of the former it may be said that he was a self-denying, sincere man, and most conscientious in every detail of duty. Of the second, John Austin Merrick, I cannot speak too strongly in the way of commendation. He was but twenty-two years of age, but he seemed thirty in maturity of mind and scholarship. He was proficient in Greek, Latin, Hebrew, and Sanscrit, and in French and Spanish also. Above all, he was a student and a strong theologian. When not on active missionary duty he was at his desk from nine in the morning until ten or eleven at night. He was a good preacher and his frequent lectures attracted attention. He was short in stature and stout, and wore a full beard, and had a solid head full of all sorts of information. One day in the year 1862 he fell in an epileptic fit, which was repeated at intervals until his mind lost its clearness. He afterwards took a parish in Kentucky, and finally went to California with Dr. Breck in 1869. I have always felt that he would have been an ornament to Church scholarship, and that his early taking off was for the Church a real misfortune. These were the men, to say nothing of the boy, who founded the mission in St. Paul.

It was the 30th of June, 1850, that the first service was held in a schoolhouse in St. Paul. The week following, four acres of land were purchased on the first rise of ground back of the centre of the town, and about half a mile from the river. Here a Sibley tent, loaned from the fort, was pitched. Dr. Geer was one of the four of us who sought rest, but found little, in that tent the first night. As Dr. Geer was large, lame, and also an elderly man, he must have found his hard couch a strong contrast to his own comfortable bed in his snug quarters at Fort Snelling. I remember he said that "for the whole mission he would not try it again." We continued to occupy the tent for two months, until a small house, twelve by sixteen feet, was enclosed, into which we moved with great thankfulness.

From the first, all domestic duties were looked after chiefly by Mr. Wilcoxson and myself. He did the cooking, and the washing fell to my lot, as I was the only experienced hand. I had learned the trade at Nashotah, having there served on the washing committee, with other distinguished men, for the better part of a year. Dr. Breck occasionally assisted at the washtub, but he could not iron a collar or shirt, to save him!

It was always a characteristic of St. Paul that everything about it was citified. It was never, even in its infancy, a village. Its buildings had an air about them which said, respect us! There was an aristocracy—a 400—clearly defined. From the beginning there was an upper and a lower town, with a strong rivalry in hotels and churches; always a struggle for commercial and social supremacy. Three large hotels were built and burned in the upper town and three in the lower town, a singular coincidence. The former was represented by such men as Governor Ramsey, Hons. Edward and Henry M. Rice, Lawyers Hollingshead and Becker, and the present Senator Judge Nelson, also John Irvine who was rich in real estate; while the lower town was represented by the American Fur Company, including a large and rich French contingent; Borup and Oaks and Robert being prominent. Yes, St. Paul was always a city, and is to-day the richest city of its size in the United States. Its banking capital is equal to that of all the rest of the State combined, although its long-time rival, Minneapolis, leads it in population.

In 1850 Minnesota seemed to be very much nearer the Arctic Circle than it does now. It was a question whether the ordinary cereals would ripen in the short summer, and the winters were intensely cold. The river was not open for navigation before the last of April, so that for about six months of the year the frozen river was the only highway, and the sleigh for three hundred miles was the only means of communication with the outer world. Few sections of our country have been more isolated in their early history than St. Paul.

The climate of Minnesota was regarded from the first as a great tonic for consumptives, and many who sought there a restoration to health, found it in the oxygen of its dry atmosphere. But more died of reckless exposure than were relieved. As an illustration, it is said there was a cavalry company formed of twenty-five invalids from the American House, who pledged themselves to appear each day ready for a ride; this was in the winter of 1855. All these were either buried there or their remains sent home to their friends. And yet the climate of St. Paul was good for some sensible people, and is to this day.

## CHAPTER XI

### THE ASSOCIATE MISSION IN ST. PAUL—CONTINUED

As soon as we were fairly in the new house, Dr. Breck set in motion the machinery of the new Nashotah. The faculty was organized with himself as president and the Rev. John A. Merrick secretary and professor of all branches. I, as the only student, constituted the college. The household, except Professor Merrick, retired at ten o'clock, and all rose at 5 A. M., and answered to our names. The first roll call was made from the region of Dr. Breck's corner, and was answered readily, as we each had a cot in the same Gothic roofed chamber, and so were within easy hearing distance. The second call was at six o'clock to Morning Prayer, a full service, then breakfast according to Wilcoxson, which, because of his inexperience, was not always a success. The faculty met once a month, or as the exigencies of the occasion might require. As a hen scratches as diligently for one chick as for ten, so one student will sometimes try a faculty more than a full contingent. What with the washing and the running of errands, and going for the mail, and other things, such as the frequent absence of both the president and secretary on missionary duty, it was a wonder how the institution kept on its feet. The laws of the college were honored more often in the breach than in the observance. Sometimes from untoward conditions there was a temporary suspension of every function of the institution, but when the clergy returned and a quorum could be secured, there was held a lengthy and solemn session of the faculty, and I would be summoned to hear the result. A new order would be posted, hours of study and recitation designated, and then the college would resume its course. The intention was serious, but the doctrine of impenetrability was against success, for no student could possibly be a general factotum and a whole college at one and the same time. No man but Dr. Breck would have attempted to realize an ideal under such untoward conditions.

Afterwards, in 1851, another young man joined us, Stephen Green Hayward, the younger brother of the one mentioned in a former chapter, and with his assistance the college assumed double proportions. His coming was a great relief to my rather lonely life and heavy responsibilities.

A small church edifice was soon erected in St. Paul, where Sunday services and one week-day night service were regularly held. The mission was poorly equipped in a musical way, as not one of the clergy could turn a tune, and there were no singers among our eight communicants, which was the strength of the parish of Christ church at its organization. This defect led me to attend a singing school twice a week during the winter of 1850. I learned some long, common, and short metre tunes, the *Gloria in Excelsis*, and two or three Gregorian and double chants. We had not even a melodeon to help us. George Nichols and myself constituted the first choir in Minnesota. On the occasion of Bishop Kemper's first visit, I recall it well, we attempted great things, but signally failed through panic and the sudden collapse of our soprano. We had secured the assistance of the "Halstead Brothers," carpenters and instrumental amateurs, and two ladies. The violin, flute and bass viol were all in tune, but in the middle of the duet we went to pieces. The instruments, however, had come to stay, and afterwards did good service in the sanctuary, to my infinite relief and delight. Of course I held all the minor offices in those days. I was chorister, Sunday-school superintendent, sexton, lay-reader, and student. Also at the house, errand boy, washerman, and general factotum.

At this time regular or occasional services had been commenced at several points: at St. Anthony, nine miles; Stillwater, fifteen miles; Willow River and Hudson, eighteen miles; Point Douglas and Hastings, thirty miles, and Cottage Grove, twelve miles. Visits were made to Sauk Rapids, fifty miles up the Mississippi, and to Taylor's Falls, on the St. Croix, about the same distance. The expense of transportation to these points would have been a large item in the cash accounts, but this difficulty was avoided neatly by deciding to itinerate. This saved our bank account by a large sum. So enamored were they of this short cut to opulence that even free rides were at a discount. These men endured hardness cheerfully, as good soldiers of Jesus Christ. The Church in Minnesota was founded in self-denial, which accounts in part, certainly, for its sturdy strength to-day. There were no railroads or bicycles then, but Dr. Breck could tackle forty miles a day on foot and win every time. Brother Wilcoxson was good for thirty, but eighteen or twenty satisfied John A. Merrick and myself. Sometimes I was obliged to meet an emergency in the capacity of lay-reader.

The Associate Mission came to a close in June, 1852, after a very successful struggle of two years. The Rev. Mr. Wilcoxson succeeded Dr. Breck as rector of Christ church, St. Paul, Mr. Merrick went East, and Dr. Breck organized his missions to the Indians at Crow Wing and Gull Lake. Why Dr. Breck sought a new field for his energies is told in a few words: Bishop Kemper refused his consent to the establishment of another theological school in the sparsely populated Northwest. He thought it premature, and that it might greatly weaken Nashotah by diverting the interest of its friends. It was doubtless a wise decision for all concerned, at that time.

Before closing this chapter on life at the mission, I wish to add a few facts which may interest the practical mind of to-day. First, as to the real estate. Dr. Breck, within a week of our landing at Fort Snelling, had purchased two acres of ground on the first range of hills back of St. Paul, from a Frenchman, Vitel Guerin by name, for which he paid fifty dollars an acre. This was shortly afterwards increased by two back acres at forty dollars each. To these first four acres three acres more were added in a little time; altogether, seven acres in the present centre of the city, for the meagre sum of a few hundred dollars. If it had remained intact until now its value would have been easily half a million. The small part still unsold belongs to the Church, and is valued at $100,000. The cheapness of this property in 1850 indicates clearly how very new and crude and wild the Northwest was at that early day. The first building erected was sixteen by twelve feet, with pointed roof. An addition twelve feet square, a few months later was added for the kitchen and dining-room. In the summer of 1851 another building was put up, in style and size a counterpart of the first, facing north. At this time, also, a parish schoolhouse was built near by, and a teacher secured in a Captain Craig, a Scotch seaman. This school was in very good form, as I recall it, but how it was that the teacher did not notice the absence of a rosy-cheeked miss one day for the space of an hour, I never could quite understand.

A few words about the first families of Christ church, St. Paul, may not be amiss before closing this section of our story. History says there were eight communicants. I remember well there were two principal families and some others. There was Judge Lambert, his wife and mother, and three children. They lived opposite the little church, corner of Third and Cedar Streets. These appeared all to be staunch Churchmen and unusually intelligent people, with a large streak of sentiment, however, especially in the wife. A Roman Catholic Sister stepped in, then a priest, then books were furnished. Mrs. Lambert caught the infection. Then all fell in line and went to Rome together, a great loss to our small flock, as one might infer. Then there was the family of John Irvine. I shall never forget the hospitality of this family or their friendship for the homesick boy who lived with three clergymen at the mission on the hill. There were five daughters and one son who broke his mother's heart by dying early. Three of the girls were old enough to be in the Sunday-school, and these, with the three children of Judge Lambert, constituted the first Sunday-school of our Church in Minnesota. The Lambert defection took away half the original school, but still the school prospered, and at the end of the year was more than twenty strong. A day of small things, indeed, but not to be despised. Mrs. Irvine was always a staunch Churchwoman, and died at a good age. All her five daughters are married, and several of them are well known in the best society of St. Paul.

Our next chapter will treat of the new mission, our first mission to the Indians west of the Mississippi River.

## CHAPTER XII

#### THE JOURNEY TO THE INDIAN MISSION

The objective point for which we started was Gull Lake, about one hundred and seventy-five miles from St. Paul. In order to reach it we walked to Minneapolis, *nee* St. Anthony Falls; then by a small steamer to Sauk Rapids, and from there by stage to Fort Ripley. There was nothing strange or startling in this journey. We stopped over night at the Fort and enjoyed the hospitality of the Rev. Solon W. Maney, then chaplain of the post, and who afterwards became a professor at Faribault, under Bishop Whipple.

The following day we were driven, seven miles, to Crow Wing. We were joined on our way by a large, dark Indian, Enmegahbowh, or Johnson, by name, who was to be our guide and interpreter. He informed us that Hole-in-the-day, Po-go-nay-ke-shick, was expecting us, not at Gull Lake, but at what was known as the Government Farm, about seven miles out from Crow Wing. This was news to Dr. Breck, and as our wagon was ordered direct to Gull Lake it proved to be very inconvenient. But Enmegahbowh advised that we obey the summons, otherwise we might offend his highness, Hole-in-the-day, and so after much discussion it was decided we must, as we could, take the Farm on our way to Gull Lake and find out what the meaning of the new orders should be. Our party at this time consisted of Dr. Breck, Captain Craig, Hayward, Holcombe, and Halstead, a carpenter by trade; and with our guide, Enmegahbowh, in all six, quite a force had we been armed. We were entering a wilderness country, twenty miles from the nearest white inhabitant, with the exception of the government blacksmith, Mr. Stapler, who with his Indian wife lived in the only house at Gull Lake, and yet there was not a gun or a knife, for protection in case of any emergency, in all our party, save my own single-barreled pistol. The day we left the fort even that was lost, and, (as I believe) Dr. Breck was responsible for its disappearance. At Crow Wing we crossed to the west side of the Mississippi and then traveled out seven miles to the Farm, where we found Po-go-nay-ke-shick, the chief, and several Indian families encamped. These people had come there to plant corn and beans on the hundred acres of ground plowed and prepared for them every year by men employed by the government for this purpose. We were none of us pleased with the location. We soon learned through our interpreter the reason for this change of base. He told us that Hole-in-the-day had really no influence with the Indians at Gull Lake; that they had their own local chiefs and that Hole-in-the-day's band was located near Crow Wing and on the Mississippi, hence his idea of getting us settled within his own territory. As Dr. Breck, after looking over the ground, was not at all satisfied with the situation, and as he had started for Gull Lake, he determined at all hazards to go there. We remained at the Farm from Thursday until the Monday following, living on what we had in our bucket and a few potatoes bought from the white men at work in the field. I think if Hole-in-the-day had provided an Indian dog-feast at the time we were so hungry, and had made an after-dinner-speech in favor of that spot for the mission, he would have shown himself a skilled diplomat, and possibly carried his point of persuading us to remain. As it was, however, the hunger increased our discontent, and so on Monday morning a conference was held and it was then decided that to Gull Lake we would go if it cost us our scalps.

On the Saturday before this it was proposed to erect a church for the next day's (Sunday) service. As there was an abundance of small pines in the vicinity, we built the church, chancel and all, and when completed we named it "St. John's in the Wilderness." We had the full service and a sermon on the parable of the Lost Sheep. At the close of the service, while standing at the entrance or porch, I noticed an Indian pick from a twig of pine a small piece of cotton, then holding it up, he said to Johnson, with an amused look on his face: "See! wool from the lost sheep." This was the interpretation to us, and illustrated admirably the wit of the Indian.

Monday morning Hayward and myself were invited by Hole-in-the-day to breakfast. I always felt that this discrimination in our favor was intended as a snub to Dr. Breck, because he had refused to remain, and was about to start for Gull Lake. The repast was served in the wigwam of the chief by two of his three wives, and consisted of bacon, fried, a hot short-cake, and a cup of tea without milk. Although simple fare it seemed a feast after our diet of three days with an ever-recurring menu of roast potatoes.

We started for Gull Lake Monday, at 10 o'clock A. M., and arrived there at 1 P. M.; a distance of eleven miles. It was a somewhat exciting journey, with many a backward look, for even Enmegahbowh, our guide, thought we might be followed by the Indians. About noon we reached Gull River, a rapid stream, and as there was no bridge or ferry we were obliged to strip, and hold our clothing above our heads while we waded, waist deep, through the rushing waters. At one o'clock we arrived at the house of Mr. Stapler, the blacksmith referred to, and soon sat down to a meal of corn beef, boiled potatoes, and good home-made bread, not omitting a refreshing cup of tea. But we were not yet out of the woods of anxiety. Dr. Breck had met Hole-in-the-day in St. Paul and supposed him to be the head chief at Gull Lake; but when we arrived it was found that the Indians there were entirely independent of him, and that they had no knowledge of us or the proposed mission. Our coming was like an invasion, and there was for a time considerable doubt whether we would be permitted to remain. It was a fortunate thing for us that just then, a Great Medicine Dance was being held there, and that many Indians from other bands were present as delegates or visitors. Shortly after noon of that first day a council was summoned of the Gull Lake chiefs and medicine men and our case was duly presented by Dr. Breck. The council chamber was the unfloored log cabin of an Indian by the name of Little Hill. It was Hobson's choice, however, as it was the only house except Stapler's in that vicinity. We all, about twenty-five, sat round in a circle against the wall, and the "pipe of peace" was solemnly passed until even Dr. Breck was obliged to draw a whiff or two, "which was against the rule" with him. The speeches concluded, we withdrew to Stapler's, where we waited anxiously two good hours, until sunset, before a decision was reached respecting the mission. The outcome being in our favor at last, we greatly rejoiced, and at once set out to pitch our tent on the shore of Gull Lake, half a mile away.

The first night in camp was not without interruption. There were four of us to occupy one small Sibley tent. Dr. Breck retired early and first, then Hayward, then Halstead, then myself, fortified with a hatchet only, my small pistol having strangely disappeared, as noted, a few days previous. I tied up the door flaps, and with the hatchet handy went on guard in a recumbent position. From experience of Indians in my youth, I knew something of their habits, and when about two o'clock, footsteps were heard in the distance approaching, I felt instinctively they were Indians, and I also knew they were not hostiles, although I was a little nervous. I determined that the sleepers should share in the coming surprise, and so when our visitors were passing the side of the tent I nudged my next neighbor, and in a low but distinct voice called: "Halstead! Indians! Indians!" The effect can be imagined. He cried out lustily, and in an instant Dr. Breck's tall figure was erect at the end of the tent, as were the other two. Meanwhile, I had begun a parley with the old Indian and his squaw, who had come to seek relief from a toothache, "only this and nothing more," but it was a good joke on them, and I had my revenge for being left to close the tent and guard the door. Although no harm came to us that night, yet I have always thought common prudence dictated that we should have delayed our occupation of the future mission ground for at least a day. It seemed a part of Dr. Breck's character to ignore difficulties and go straight to the mark. I think he really did not wish to see dangers if there were any. His persistence was such, in any course he decided upon, that nothing but a stone wall would stop him. It is not improbable that he regarded himself as an apostle sent, and that nothing would be permitted to hurt him while in the way of duty.

## CHAPTER XIII

### THE INDIAN MISSION

BAD-BOY, our nearest neighbor and a chief of standing and influence, seemed to be the canoe-builder for his band. He had a wife and two daughters, and all lived in one birch-bark wigwam, about twelve by eighteen feet in size. The women were cleanly in person and excellent housekeepers, and usually had enough to meet their daily needs. I suppose this was really a good type of the best families. I observed that the older members were industrious, especially the women. Now and then the larder became empty; this happened, I should say, about once in two weeks, and then there would be a scattering in search of food. The wife would go to Crow Wing, twelve miles, for a bag of flour; the son-in-law started out with his young squaw on a hunting expedition; Bad-Boy went after fish, and Wanequance, Cloud-Woman, the youngest, gathered huckleberries and red raspberries, which grew in abundance, and traded them with us for hot soda biscuits. On the third day all were at home again with their fish and game and flour. Then there was a feast, a single dish of several ingredients, and every one had a panful; I regret now that I did not sample it that I might speak more intelligently of its merits. Then, after that, the fare became moderate; then scarce; then they endured the pangs of hunger until it drove them again to the woods and lakes for supplies.

The young and unmarried appear to enjoy life after much the same fashion as do those of a fairer skin. There is courting and flirting, the accredited beauty, and the genuine fop or dude who, like his white namesake, is generally an idler. There was an Indian maiden, I remember, a visitor from a distant tribe. Gamwanabequa was her musical name. She was indeed a real beauty, of the Indian type. I could not describe her, or the charm she exercised over others. As I recall, she had a fine, rich complexion, small feet and hands, regular features, and white, even teeth that gleamed in a well-cut mouth. Her hair was very abundant, and, above all, her eyes were soft and expressive, a dimple or two emphasized the sweetest of smiles. This young squaw had always two or three young men about her, whom she delighted to tantalize. After stopping long enough to break a heart or two, Miss Gamwanabequa left for her distant home, and we saw her no more.

The Indian dude or fop is also a distinct species. About once a week he makes a most elaborate toilet. He has his kit, which includes combs, a hand glass, hair grease and paints—red, yellow, green, and black—and ribbons. When this young man desires to get himself into his best form, he does not "seek the seclusion which his cabin grants," but the most conspicuous position possible. He sits down at the base of a tree, where, for an hour, he is so absorbed in making himself beautiful that it is almost impossible to distract his attention. He combs and oils and braids his long locks, and then summons all his energies to secure an absolutely straight part in the very centre of his head, which he proceeds to color with red paint. Then, with glass in hand, he makes up his face as his fancy suggests. He tackles his complexion first, and having secured the most approved tint, he proceeds with the decoration in black, blue, red, and yellow, and when all this part of his toilet is completed he ties a ribbon on the end of each braid; scrutinizes himself carefully in his mirror, and, with a grunt of satisfaction, arranges his blanket becomingly, and struts forth like a wild turkey cock to exhibit his points. The vanity of the fellow is unspeakable; his coxcombry, flamboyant; his self-adulation, supreme; he poses, he nips, he winks, he casts eyes at the young maidens who admire while they laugh at his conceit. No, indeed, the modern dude, licking his cane, is "not in it" with this primitive man of the forest. He is but a poor imitator of an earlier type—a case of devolution rather than evolution. The species is evidently in its decadence, for which the world may well be congratulated.

With reference to birch canoes and their construction, I said that Bad-Boy was the only manufacturer at Gull Lake. He constructed two or three every summer; and I will say that his canoes were unexcelled for strength and model. There is certainly no floating beauty, unless it be the swan, which compares for grace of outline with a birch canoe fresh from the hands of such an artist as our chief at Gull Lake. "It is a thing of beauty and a joy forever." I witnessed the construction of three. Bad-Boy with three squaws and two canoes, crossed the lake, and was absent four or five days, when he returned laden with material for three canoes of average size. The material for a canoe consists of birch bark, white ash or hickory for ribs, and white wood or basswood for lining, with roots for wrapping or sewing, besides pine pitch for rendering the seams impervious to water. The model of the canoe appears to be only in the mind of the builder. I should say that it required about three weeks to complete two canoes. No hand touches the growing beauty save that of the Master. When completed it is a work of art without flaw or blemish. I will note the one exception to the above rule: When the canoe is nearly completed, the squaws take a hand, and have a regular quilting bee, as it were, sitting on either side of the canoe; eight or ten, altogether.

They wrap, with roots, the upper rim of the boat, round and round from end to end, piercing the bark below the strips for the root to pass through. The Indian women laugh and chatter on these occasions, with as evident enjoyment as their pale-faced sisters. Given a like environment, and human nature is much the same, whether the color of the skin be white or red.

## CHAPTER XIV

### THE INDIAN MISSION—CONTINUED

In the space of a week from the time when we located on Gull Lake, about twenty birch wigwams had been set up around us, forming quite a community. Captain Craig now opened his school for small Indians on a bench, back of a wooden shanty where our cooking was done and our frugal meals eaten. It was the duty of Hayward and myself to look after the culinary department, alternating a week about. Meanwhile, Halstead, our carpenter, was getting out logs for the house, assisted by Hayward or myself, a week in turn, as our domestic affairs permitted.

There was but one further interruption to our peace, which, however, we were not altogether unprepared for. We suspected that Hole-in-the-day's anger would not be appeased until he had made one effort, at least, to drive us away. It was about the second week when we learned that he had arrived at Gull Lake with a part of a keg of whiskey. We were then convinced that he intended to get the Indians drunk and persuade them to violence. We learned afterwards that he did call a council, and deliver an incendiary speech, but his mission proved a dead failure and thenceforth our scalps were safe.

From the honorable treatment we received at the hands of the Gull Lake chiefs, I have since concluded that the "dead Indian is not the only good Indian," as some people, consulting their prejudices, seem to think. Of course there are Indians and Indians. The Ojibway cannot be understood, nor his mode of living compared, with the Winnebago or the Sioux. They are as unlike as the men of Ohio and Western Tennessee. The Sioux live on the plains, and in a dirty skin tepe; the Ojibway in a wigwam of birch bark, than which nothing is cleaner. The Indian of the woods and the lakes is generally a better specimen of a man than the Indian of the prairie and plains. The Sax and Foxes of Illinois and Iowa were very intelligent, and lived by farming in summer and hunting in winter, while the Winnebagoes were no better than tramps and existed by stealing from better people. Any wholesale denunciation of the red man as such, indicates both ignorance and prejudice. Bad-Boy and White Eagle, the two principal chiefs at Gull Lake, were men of intelligence and serenity. They were the heads of families well governed. They would scorn a mean or shady act as beneath their dignity. These men had no use for Hole-in-the-day, as they well understood his cruel, tricky nature, and indignantly resented his attempted interference in matters connected with the mission of Dr. Breck, and within their own proper jurisdiction.

## The Indian Mission—Continued

It is agreed that environment has much to do with shaping the destiny of a race. The men of the mountains are more patriotic than the men of the plain. The Indian is the natural man. He knows nothing of literature, nothing of the sciences. In his natural state the Ojibway Indian is a truth teller and stands by his word. This trait is preeminent with him, but is contrary to the experience of King David who says that "all men are liars," the most common of all sins of the civilized races to-day. The wars of the natural man are cruel, and always have been. The captive had no rights and no claim upon his adversary. The sentiment of pity is a cultivated sentiment, and was unknown in the world until the coming of Christ. How then could we expect to find it in the breast of the uneducated, unchristianized Indian? The Indian of this country will become valuable as a citizen just in proportion to his Christian possibilities. It is a fact that to-day the only Indians advancing in civilization are those under Christian influence, make of it what we will.

The mission at Gull Lake owes its importance chiefly to the fact that it was the first one established by our Church for the Indians, west of the Mississippi. A great deal has been done for the Indians by Bishop Whipple and Bishop Hare since 1859, the date of the former's consecration; but this mission broke the ground for all that was to follow in Minnesota and beyond to the

Pacific coast. The first venture is the trial venture. Dr. Breck had the courage to enter new and untried fields, unbacked by money or pledges, relying solely on himself and his own ability to furnish all necessary supplies. He did not send an agent to the East for means. Whatever the mail brought day by day was his only dependence. Dr. Breck, as far as I know, took no one into his financial confidence. He neither complained nor rejoiced at the fortunes of a day. His serenity was not affected by the state of his bank account. I never heard him say he was anxious or discouraged. In all conditions, like St. Paul, he had learned to be content.

To continue the story of the two months, July and August, 1852, during which the log house was completed, Dr. Breck spent a good part of this time away from the mission. He went to St. Paul twice at least, and was absent ten days or two weeks each time, and occupied a room at Mr. Stapler's when at the mission. When he left St. Paul he left all the traditions and uses which characterized the journey to St. Paul and the life at the mission there. For us young men, it was no more than a summer outing. We were on the shore of a very beautiful lake, six miles long and three wide. We soon became accustomed to the birch canoe and spent much of our leisure time in swimming or canoeing.

## CHAPTER XV

### A CANOE TRIP

WE remained at the mission through July and August of 1852, and then, the small log house being completed, we were ready to return to St. Paul, leaving Captain Craig as the sole representative until Dr. Breck should get back. To save expense, it was determined that we should go to St. Paul by water in a birch canoe. We secured a second-hand one for five dollars that would carry four comfortably. Hayward and myself had mastered the birch canoe by the constant practice of two months, and felt capable of making the journey by water, although as yet we had not tried our skill in the strong current of a river. The weak point in a birch canoe is its bottom. On the deep waters of the lake you are safe, for it will ride any billow like a swan; but in river travel there are shallows and rocks and logs and sharp limbs of fallen trees, and to run full on or against any of these is to puncture or scrape a hole in the bark, and then you must get to shore quickly or be submerged. Any ordinary injury, however, is readily mended with pitch pine gum, which every canoeist carries for just such emergencies. As Dr. Breck and Halstead had little experience with the paddle, they were readily excused from a contribution of their inexperience, and became practically cabin passengers. Hayward, at the bow, was lookout and paddler, while I, at the stern, was supposed to assist in the labor and direct the course of the canoe.

The journey by water to St. Anthony Falls was about two hundred miles, which we accomplished in three days, but not without incident and some adventure. Our Indian friends witnessed our departure with many expressions of regret, and on our part it was responded to most earnestly, if not tearfully. Dr. Breck, they knew, would soon return, but for us, they realized, as did we, that we should see each other no more in this life forever. Gull Lake, or Kahgeeashkoonsikag, is one of three lakes; the other two are known as Round Lake and Long Lake; all of these empty their waters through the Gull and Crow Wing Rivers into the Mississippi, a distance of about fifty-three miles, and by land direct, as the crow flies, eighteen miles; yet we accomplished by canoe the fifty-three miles between 10 A. M. and 7 P. M. A birch canoe, to one not accustomed to its ways, is as restive and dangerous as an unbroken colt or a bicycle. It did not occur to me at the time, but as I look back upon that journey of two hundred miles in the low waters of August, I think I did exceed-

## A Canoe Trip

ingly well to bring my crew and passengers safely to the end of the voyage.

The first day took us six miles to the foot of Gull Lake; then forty miles to the Mississippi; then seven miles down the Mississippi landed us at Fort Ripley, where we stopped to say goodbye to the Rev. Mr. Maney, the chaplain who had entertained us so hospitably on our way up. It was here that Dr. Breck felt called upon to assume command of the canoe, although, in fact, it belonged to Hayward and myself, for we had paid five dollars for it, while he had declined to contribute. Dr. Breck made many inquiries of the officers of the Fort about the river below, and so insisted on an opinion as to the safer side that finally one of them, who knew really nothing about it, responded that the left was probably the safer side. I felt really indignant at this assumption of authority, and quietly determined that I should be governed entirely by my own judgment. This brought on, very soon, a conflict of authority. We had not gone a mile before the current changed from the east to the west side, and, naturally, I followed the current to keep off the shallows. "Where are you going now?" asked the new captain, in a tone of earnest interrogation. "The officer advised the east side as the safer." I responded that I was at the helm and alone responsible, and cared nothing for the officer's advice, unless it happened to agree with the trend of the current and my best judgment. After this, Dr. Breck subsided into silence, as he always did when he had no power to enforce his orders.

That day we ran Pike Rapids and over a fall of about ten feet successfully. We were very much elated at this, but, as we discovered later on, it was a small affair in comparison with what we were to encounter on the morrow. Fifty miles above Minneapolis is an island dividing the river, and on its east side there are tumbling, rushing rapids about three-fourths of a mile in length. We arrived at this interesting spot about ten o'clock in the morning. Half a mile above the rapids I inquired of a man who stood on the bank watching us, whether the Indians were accustomed to run the rapids, and he answered that he had never made the venture himself, but that the Indians sometimes did in high water. As it was now August, and the water, as usual at that time of year, very low, our spirits were much depressed. Dr. Breck declared it madness to think of it. When we had brought the canoe to shore, he and Halstead got out and took all their belongings with them. I remember that Dr. Breck remarked he would not trust even his old boots if we decided to risk our lives in the attempt. The alternative for Hayward and myself was that we must run the rapids or make a portage of about a mile. To carry the canoe that distance was a serious matter, and we had no mind to it, so we consulted and talked it over for a time; then we went down some distance on the bank and looked the rapids over. We noted that the main body of the stream held well together in the middle of the river for a considerable distance; then a mighty current shot off to the right bank, where it met a low reef of rocks, which sent it off again to the left shore; then all connections were lost in the rush and foam of it. That was all we could see or know. We seemed already to have decided that this was but a preliminary act, for we had no further discussion, but jumped into the canoe, pushed out from the shore, and followed the main shoot as we had observed it, so committing ourselves to whatever fortune the next ten minutes had in store for us. It was doubtless a risky adventure, but the excitement and the rush of it, and the glorious leaps and shoots of the canoe, were a delight beyond all words. We went easily and steadily, swifter and swifter, for a hundred yards; then we were flung to the right, and seemed to be plunging on to the reef; then we were swirled about, and driven with a mighty current to the east, and then we were in a jumble of waves, tossed up and down, until at length, the danger passed, we glided swiftly on and into the smoother water, and soon drew our good canoe on shore in safety. There were but two or three marks of the struggle visible; and long before Dr. Breck and Halstead joined us, we had mended our craft and were quietly smoking our pipes of tobacco and kinikanick, enjoying the unspent sensations of our exciting ride. As it was a hot day, our friends were very tired and perspiring with their long walk, while we were fresh and triumphant. The canoe journey closed at six o'clock that evening, with a large leak in the bottom of our bark from lifting it over the logs of a boom just above St. Anthony Falls, and Hayward and myself were completely drenched by the inrushing water. We drew the canoe up under an old warehouse, by the river, and walked down to St. Paul, nine miles, and so completed our journey.

This concludes the hitherto unwritten history of the founding of the first Indian mission of our Church west of the Mississippi River. The exposure to which Hayward and myself were subjected resulted in a short run of bilious fever for my part, but with my friend it was far more serious. We both returned to Nashotah in September of that year, 1852, and shortly afterwards Hayward came down with a very serious attack of typhoid fever, which left him with a lung affection from which he died a few years later. Samuel Josiah Hayward, the older brother, took the fever from nursing Stephen, from which he never fully recovered. He also died of consumption in a little time, and was buried at Nashotah. The death of these two stalwart men is to be traced directly to the founding of the Gull Lake mission. Were these men martyrs?

## CHAPTER XVI

### THE PROVIDENTIAL MAN

BEFORE closing these personal reminiscences, I wish to go back a little and explain more fully the beginnings of this Indian mission, and in so doing, I shall be able to give the credit to that providential man, Enmegahbowh; for, after all, it was to him and through him that our first Indian mission in the far West came to be thought of and finally undertaken. It must have been in the fall of 1851 that Enmegahbowh attended the annual payment of his tribe, at Fort Snelling, and it was here that he met for the first time a clergyman of our Church.

Enmegahbowh had learned to speak English in Canada. At the age of sixteen he came to the Chippeways, in the Territory of Minnesota. For a time he acted as interpreter to a Methodist minister, but he was not satisfied with their methods for the Indian. After conversation with him, Dr. Geer, our chaplain at the fort, gave him a prayer-book. The prayer-book made him a churchman, and he at once, through Dr. Geer, opened a correspondence with Dr. Breck, and earnestly represented the great opportunity there was for a mission of the Church to the Indians.

The result of Enmegahbowh's efforts was that arrangements were soon made for Dr. Breck to visit Gull Lake and confer with Hole-in-the-day —the traditional war chief of the Chippeways. The last and pressing argument for the visit was that Hole-in-the-day was very ill and likely to die of dangerous wounds he had received, and that it was all important that Dr. Breck should meet him and consult about the proposed mission while there was an opportunity. Upon receipt of this letter from Enmegahbowh, Dr. Breck arranged to start at once for Gull Lake.

It was about the 10th of February, 1852, that Dr. Breck, with Stephen Green Hayward, the other divinity student, as his traveling companion, set out on this journey of 132 miles in the wilderness. In a letter written to his brother at this time, Dr. Breck says: "Think of this, my brother! The Romish bishop but a short time since spent two hours in his wigwam (*i. e.*, Hole-in-the-day's) trying to persuade him to be baptized, and the brave warrior refuses; not for unbelief in Christianity, for Hole-in-the day desires to be taught, but by reason of the *system*, which his father, a noble chief before him, refused. The head chief rejects the plausible system of Rome, and asks for the Catholic system of the Church. Such is the nature of the door that is opening to us, and is it possible for us to refuse to enter? The knock is given, we must open." And then he adds: "I have just walked 115 miles through a country but little inhabited, in order to gratify the wishes of this influential chief."

I do not think we have heretofore stated the fact distinctly that the Indian mission was started under the auspices of the original associate mission, located at St. Paul. Dr. Breck always saw a finality in every enterprise he started; so now he felt that he was to spend the rest of his life in the Indian field. He was a man who always entertained the largest ideas; without a dollar in bank he founded universities and organized associate missions—and now, in imagination, he beheld St. Columba the centre of a field extending to the Red River of the North, and west to the line of the Dakotas; and possibly he saw also, as in a vision, a future Indian diocese, and the episcopate crowning all. In 1852 Dr. Breck was in the very prime of his life, and to such a man, believing all things, hoping all things, all things were possible. The enthusiasm of his youth was only tempered by the years of his varied experience, and so he turned from the bitter disappointment at St. Paul as if it had been but a passing cloud, and plunged into the struggle of the wilderness, challenging all his tried and veteran supporters to enter with him and reap the rich fields already whitening to the harvest. It is interesting to note the circumstance that just at this time the Romanists and Presbyterians were striving to gain a foothold for missions also, and these last had already planted themselves at the Indian Farm—a location which Dr. Breck had already seen and rejected. Dr. Breck was so thoroughly satisfied with Gull Lake as a centre for schools and missionary work, that he declared he would prefer it with only $1,000 a year to the Presbyterian outlook at the Farm with its $5,000.

Dr. Breck regarded every new field as a finality. With him, Nashotah and St. Paul and Faribault were all finalities. "Man proposes, but God disposes." He imagined, also, at this time that Hole-in-the-day—who was repentant because he was sick—was to be the man through whom the door was to be held open by which he could safely enter this new field of labor for the Indian. But, as we have seen, Hole-in-the-day proved only a broken reed when the day of trial came. "When the devil was sick, the devil a monk would be; when the devil was well, the devil a monk was he." Hole-in-the-day's life proved him both treacherous and cruel. With his own hand he had killed two Indians in drunken brawls, and he himself, some years later, was shot and killed, while riding in his buggy from Crow Wing to the farm, and by a relative of one of these men whom he had murdered.

I think I said once before that Hole-in-the-day, by traffic with the whites had become a man of

## The Providential Man

some considerable means, but I did not say that he had a winter house near Gull Lake, built of hewn logs, and that it was in this palace, as Dr. Breck called it, that Hole-in-the-day lay sick at the time when he first visited him, in February, 1852.

This account of the beginning of things makes it clear that Enmegahbowh, the good Indian, was the providential man who had been raised up for this initiatory work. In 1859, Sunday, July 3d, at Faribault, Minn., after five years of preparation and in the thirty-sixth year of his life, Enmegahbowh was ordained, with two others, to the diaconate by Bishop Kemper. This was the first ordination, and this was also the first Indian deacon of our Church, so far as I am informed at the present writing, and it is certainly true of all the tribes west of the great river. Enmegahbowh was a tower of strength to the Indian mission in all its years of trial and danger, and it was through his courage and bravery in warning the white settlers that a terrible massacre was averted in 1862. Even to this day he is the most conspicious of our Indian clergyman, and at the advanced age of ninety-three years he remains the faithful priest of his little flock, in meekness and constancy ministering to their souls' needs. I should like to speak of his faithful wife who learned to read and write that she might become an efficient helpmate to her husband. She was a woman full of faith and good works, and the sick and afflicted ever found in her a helpful friend. Enmegahbowh was the herald of all our Indian work; the man who cried from the wilderness, "Come over and help us"; the man who first opened the door for all that has since followed of God's work for the Indians, even to the Pacific Coast. Let honor be given where honor is due, and may a sense of appreciation warm his heart before the shadows fall or the sun sets upon his earthly pathway.[1]

[1] Enmegahbowh has since died.

## CHAPTER XVII

#### THE MARRIAGE OF DR. BRECK

ON All Saints' day, 1852, the corner-stone of the church of St. Columba, at Gull Lake, was laid with appropriate ceremonies. This church built of squared logs—having nave and chancel, and architecturally, of the early pointed style, was completed and consecrated the following summer by Bishop Kemper. This was the first Indian church west of the Mississippi River— of any name. The mission house had been enlarged and finished, and crowning all was the old mission bell, above the front gable of the central building. Could its iron tongue have told the story of its wanderings, it would have said: "I came from Oneida, Wis., in 1842, to Nashotah, and there I was hung and rung in a tree by the hand of Dr. Breck himself, and was always on time. I was the monitor who broke the slumbers of the Nashotah sleepers at five o'clock—I summoned them to chapel at six o'clock, and then to their daily toil at one. I tolled them joyfully the hour of rest. I rang their lights out at ten. I was again in a tree at St. Paul doing my honest work. In those days I was a wild bell, unhoused and storm-beaten; now I am in a belfry, for the first time, and feel quite at home, but still clanging—'for the tongue can no man tame,' and ringing for the astonishment and delight of these wild children of the forest. I presume they regard me as an essential part of the mission plant, and I shall be careful not to undeceive them unless my clapper fails me." By this time the mission had become quite a settlement. There must have been at least six or seven log houses built by the Indians for their own use within the first year.

1852–3 were red letter years in Dr. Breck's life. He was now past forty years of age, and still a single man, and a free man, but now for the first time a woman—of his own race and color—appeared to adorn and help and, alas! disturb the even tenor of a life which hitherto had been as a smoothly flowing river. I think, perhaps, Dr. Breck had but a faint suspicion of all it might mean for him. There was need, and a place for a matron in the household, and as the supply is usually equal to the demand, Mrs. Wells, a cultured and charming lady, obeyed the summons and crossed the mission threshold. Then others followed in rapid succession—Miss Mills and Miss Allen *et al.*, and soon Dr. Breck's family was increased to fifteen persons, not including a contingent of Indian children of both sexes. It was not a great while after this that the usual troubles began. The propinquity, the social dependence, the exhilarating atmosphere of *kahgee-ashkoon si kag*—the beauty of the moonlights, the daily association—all these, as the good doctor writes to his Bishop, "threatens love. This bringing together of a number of unmarried missionaries, both male and female, is rather more than I can manage—I have determined to marry them off as fast as I can. There is no mending of the matter in any other way." A most philosophical conclusion, nor was Dr. Breck himself entirely free from suspicion of honorable intention towards the sex he had heretofore declined to consider matrimonially, and this may account for his rapid acquiescence in the desires of others who like himself had waited and hoped in vain. It was not, however, until some time later that the "morning papers" had this announcement: "Married, on Saturday, August 11, 1855, in the church of St. Columba, near Fort Ripley, by the Rev. E. G. Geer, chaplain U. S. A., the Rev. James Lloyd Breck, missionary to the Chippeways, and Miss Jane Maria Mills, daughter of the late William R. Mills, Esq., of Argyle, New York."

This event must have been something of a shock to his admiring friends who had companied with him all the time since he left the East, and who like Aaron and Hur had on all sides held up his hands financially, but it did not seem to abate one jot of his enthusiasm for Indian missions.

In those days the culinary department was administered by one Parker, who had, I surmise, married Miss Allen, the imported mission worker referred to. From a remark once made in strict confidence by Dr. Breck, we may imagine the biscuits were not quite up to date, nor as wholesome as in those days of happy memory when Hayward and Holcombe reigned as *chefs* of the shanty. Dr. Breck, without fear of gainsaying, declared that he had eaten more salaratus in Parker's administration than in all his life before. It is but right to say just here that Parker's reign preceded that of Mrs. Breck, when doubtless all such wrongs were forgiven and forgotten.

## CHAPTER XVIII

### THE TRYING YEAR

THE year 1854, which was the second of the mission, proved, financially, a very trying one to the faith and courage of Dr. Breck. The associate mission at St. Paul was still on his hands, with many of its obligations to be met; the church at Stillwater was to be got ready for consecration on the occasion of the approaching visit of Bishop Kemper, beside the completion of the church and buildings at Gull Lake; and in addition to all this, there were the current expenses of the mission, which then consisted of a family of fourteen adults and some twenty Indian children. All this meant a very large outlay of money. Then, too, we can imagine that this new enterprise had already, in the first flush of interest, overtaxed the liberality of his friends. It was certainly to be expected that there would be a temporary lull in remittances from sheer exhaustion, and this seems to have been realized in 1854. Almost any other man would have sunk under the burden in dismay, but if any so think of Dr. Breck, he is mistaken in the man and his make-up, and just as much so in the character of the men and women who sustained his enterprises by their gifts. This year, also, was marked by troubles in connection with the property at St. Paul, the control of which Dr. Breck had transferred to other hands—a mistake he afterwards regretted, when it was too late for repentance. On the other hand, this year of clouds had its silver lining, in the good success of the mission, and especially in the first installment of $1,000 paid by the general government as a contribution to help on the education of its Indian wards. It was this offer of the government, and others following, that encouraged Dr. Breck to attempt in the near future the opening of other missions and schools at still more distant points.

It is interesting to observe how, in the history of Dr. Breck and in the founding of successive enterprises at Nashotah, St. Paul, Gull Lake, Faribault, and St. Augustin, Cal., the contributions to the new did not materially affect the support of those which preceded them. It was greatly feared by Drs. Adams and Cole—and even Bishop Kemper himself was not without serious apprehension—that in leaving Nashotah for St. Paul Dr. Breck would be followed in sympathy by all his friends in the East, greatly to the injury, if not to the actual destruction, of the income on which Nashotah depended for very existence. Dr. Breck, however, seemed to have no such apprehension. He always believed that Nashotah was needed for the education of young men for the ministry, and that God would sustain it for His own uses. He was just as confident that Minnesota required its own institutions of learning, and that Nashotah could not furnish the men necessary at an early day to occupy the towns and cities that were to spring up in a night, as it were, all over the great Northwest. His firm belief was that if men would give themselves to the work—not counting the cost—God would raise up friends to sustain them. And so it really seemed to be in all his varied experiences. For each new venture of faith new friends were created who, in their enthusiasm, almost dared him to ask more than they were willing to supply. They were indeed a noble army of strong men and noble women, and even children, who stood shoulder to shoulder with the great missionary from the days of early Nashotah until he sank exhausted with his "labors more abundant" on the Pacific coast.

Dr. Breck excelled not only in possessing the courage of his convictions, but in his power to enkindle the souls of others with a devotion similar to his own. Of this power, I think he was always conscious. As in this year of trial he stood in the presence of an empty larder, so often in times past he had faced similar conditions undismayed. Even when there was discoverable only a little flour in the bottom of the barrel with which to feed his large and dependent family, there was no outward sign of worry or anxiety. At that time two mails a week reached Fort Ripley, and these were brought to the mission by the fleet Indian runner, Gegabish, and the letters he brought that very day were white-winged messengers of peace and relief to the strong soul who could both work and wait with equal serenity; for, like the great Apostle, he might truly say: "In all things I have learned both to be filled and to be hungry; both to abound and to be in want. I can do all things through Him that strengtheneth me."

It was some time in 1853 that Dr. Breck revisited Nashotah. With the opening of the Indian country to the north and west of St Columba, he saw there would be urgent need of more workmen. Thus far Nashotah had not furnished a single man to assist him, and the East held out no hope of any recruits for the frontier. Indeed, his old-time patron and friend, Dr. Muhlenberg, urged him to abandon the field and return to New York, where, on the "East Side," perhaps, he might find a congenial corner of the vineyard for work. As well cage the eagle and clip his wings as make such an incongruous suggestion to our great missionary. The visit to Nashotah was a brief but happy one for Dr. Breck, as he received a right royal welcome from his former associates and parishioners, for it had already been demonstrated that his new enterprises had worked no harm to the mother

## The Trying Year

mission, but rather declared her importance as a school of the prophets. If Dr. Breck's visit was for the purpose of securing helpers for his Indian work, it seemed a failure; but if we count a single conversion as sometimes of more value than a thousand, then perhaps he accomplished more than he realized at the time. In 1854, the Rev. Mr. Peake, who had just received Priests' Orders, with Bishop Kemper's advice, became Nashotah's first and only contribution to the mission fields of Minnesota. Mr. Peake was a man of loyal spirit, both to Church and country, and when Dr. Breck required a successor at St. Columba that he might be free to advance his missionary outposts, he found in Mr. Peake the "man of his right hand," "the providential man" "raised up, indeed, for such a time as this."

## CHAPTER XIX

### ST. COLUMBA

The success of St. Columba mission as a civilizing agency for the Indian had already received recognition by the government authorities. The governor of the territory of Minnesota, who was then the superintendent of Indian affairs, writes Dr. Breck in January, 1854: "I am gratified to hear from all sources the unexampled success you are having in the great cause of humanity. Your mission is now, and has been, doing more than any mission I know of. It will be highly gratifying to have a detailed report from you by the last of September, that I may forward it to the government and make it a part of the future history of the red man's redemption." Could anything have been more gratifying than such official recognition?

The success and extent of the work at the end of the second year is evident. The church had been erected and the mission house completed. The average daily attendance at Morning and Evening Prayer was about fifty; some in white man's garb, many in the blanket, because of inability to secure for them what all desired. The women were taught to make their own

GEN. THEO. SEMINARY
LIBRARY

MISSION HOUSE (St. Columba).

clothes, and all the household duties were performed by them under the direction of Mrs. Breck and her assistants. The mission farm was worked by Indian laborers. In the course of the year, as many as 500 Indians had in some form taken part in the daily duties of the mission. Eighteen months before this, Bad-Boy (On'e-wash-gashish) had declared in an impassioned address that the white man desired them to work only that he might make slaves of them; now this representative wise man of his tribe lived in his own log-house and had become a regular church attendant. Dr. Breck writes at this time that there is scarcely an Indian family that has not a distinct garden under cultivation, and some of these are quite large.

Dr. Breck placed the Church's system so far above sectarian subjective methods that he felt no fears from their efforts to draw away the Indians after them, for he appreciated what the sects have never grasped—that the civilizing and Christianizing of an Indian meant the same thing; that the savage must get out of his hut and into a house, and off with his blanket and on with the white man's garb; that to feel like a man and Christian, he must have, in a word, the environment of civilization. This was Dr. Breck's theory for the treatment of the Indian, and hence his immediate success at Gull Lake. Even before our first log house was completed, in August, 1852, it had become an object lesson to the poor

Indian. With the possibility of securing tools for house building, and assisted by Dr. Breck in the selection of trees suitable for the purpose, and having been also instructed in the use of the ax and in scoring and "hewing to the line," the Indians were encouraged to go to work willingly for the first time in their idle lives. The woods resounded with a new impact, and soon became vocal with unwonted echoes as each man strove to outdo his neighbor in preparing logs for the house and home that was to be.

Dr. Breck never knew an idle waking hour; his example was ever a rebuke to the indolent and an encouragement to the self-respecting who desired to better their present condition.

Captain Craig—as related before—was the first Indian schoolmaster, and also the medicine man at the mission. His kit of tools consisted chiefly of an old-fashioned turnkey for extracting teeth; but Craig's reign ended suddenly for the reason that he administered the medical department without compunction—the frequent yells of agony issuing from the operating room behind the shanty indicated the ruthless outcome of a molar, under the vigorous manipulations of Captain Craig. *Similia similibus curantur*, or make a pain to cure a pain, was his invariable prescription. The story of our first teacher's departure is referred to by Dr. Breck in a letter written September, 1852. "Yesterday I pulled out a tooth for an old woman with signal success. I am sorry to say my Brother Craig had not sufficient of that singular virtue called prudence, and instead thereof grew excitable. I had to tell him he might be happier elsewhere, so that he has left, and the medical treatment has fallen upon myself entirely. You will judge that I am in high repute when I am called upon to minister cures to stone-blind old men and to long-standing, incurable diseases. In many cases I have been, thank God, highly successful. Were you to see me in the wretched wigwams applying liniments and rubbing their filthy persons with my hands you would really think me an Indian enthusiast, but I trust I do thereby become all things to all men to gain some."

It was just about this time the largest offering ever made, either to Nashotah or St. Paul or the Indian mission, from any source, was presented upon the Ojibway altar. It was $1,000 in gold coin—the third part only of what the general government was to give that year. The agent's expression on giving Dr. Breck the money was, that "it should be regarded as the government's appreciation of the work accomplished by the mission, and its desire to extend its usefulness." My hope from these quotations is to establish the fact that our first Indian mission in the Northwest was, from the start, a real success. When Dr. Breck went there it was a howling wilderness. The missions of other denominations, as the Methodist and Presbyterian, had failed.

There was a strong prejudice against Dr. Breck's undertaking, with many, from the first. Our first day at Gull Lake was spent in anxiety and apprehension that we would not be permitted to remain. Where we set up our tent on the lake shore there were no Indian wigwams, no beginnings of civilization; only the trees and the lake and the small tent of the great pioneer. Dr. Breck did not seem to seek these people; they came to him and set up their homes, and so made a village round about the tall white man. They came to see what he would do for them, and what it all meant for the red man. They were curious and suspicious. They were poor as poverty. They were idle and dirty and ignorant and superstitious, and as untamed and wild as the forests and lakes around them.

Now that two years have passed, all is changed; another day has dawned for the benighted savage. The desert has become a garden; the wigwam a house; the idle savage a self-respecting workman —presto! and the scene is transformed. Dr. Breck sits under his own vine and fig-tree, and his Indian children work his will and do his bidding, and are happy in the knowledge of the better way. It is this transformation scene that attracts the attention of the governor of Minnesota and wins his commendation. It is the fame of this enterprise that brings swift-footed messengers from at least seven different tribes; first, to see with their own eyes what it is all like, and then to entreat that the good and great man will visit their distant homes. Every inducement was offered; every argument exhausted to induce and persuade him to leave St. Columba in other hands, and afford them the same privileges he had given to others of their people.

The most important of these more western points was Kehsahgah, or Leech Lake, sixty miles distant, where was located a very large community of Indians, what was known as the "Pillager Band." It was to visit this place that Dr. Breck and the Rev. Solon W. Maney, with an officer of the fort, set out in the month of March, 1853, less than one year from the time the Gull Lake mission was opened. Of this thrilling journey and the future of Kehsahgah we shall tell further on.

Of the spiritual side of the work, a little later he writes: "I have had the happiness to baptize sixty-seven Chippeways. A lifelong labor opens before me in the red man's country, and I have no wish to return to the white field. I feel as perfectly at home among the aborigines as I ever did at Nashotah." On the occasion of Bishop Kemper's visit in the summer of 1855, sixteen natives, all in white garments, were confirmed. As these sixteen white garments came from Nashotah, and were used there for a class of sixteen, I have a strong feeling that one of them must have been my very own. Such a discovery is very suggestive, but I recall the fact with pleasure—that, as in the case of the wolf and the lamb, my place was farthest up the stream.

## CHAPTER XX

### KAHSAHGAH

THIS lake is situated sixty miles north of Gull Lake. It is thirty miles long and fifteen wide. Its shores are irregular with several bold promontories, and in this lake are two islands. It is the largest of all the many lakes in that section of the northwest. The water is clear and sweet, and swarms with fish, the most useful of which is known as the " white shad of the lakes." This fish, when frozen, will remain for months unchanged in quality, and is, therefore, a chief reliance of the Indian when food is scarce in winter. For the delicacy of this fish when first taken from the water, I can myself testify, and Dr. Breck was authority for its excellence in the preserved state. Kahsahgah is bordered by forests, and the sugar maple abounds on all its shores. Thousands of pounds of sugar are made every spring by the Indians, and as maple sugar is always in demand and at a good price, it was a chief source of revenue for the red man. In some sections of the country the wild rice could be gathered, a most useful article in their domestic economy. Then, in the season, there is an abundance of wild fruits, as the red raspberry, the huckleberry, the cranberry. The lakes are full of geese and ducks, and in the forests many kinds of game, large or small abound. All this nature provides for the primitive man in the northwest—the happiest of all countries for the Indian. And "yet they were not happy," in view of the more settled conditions of civilization which they beheld at St. Columba. Their thin birch houses, hot in summer, and cold in winter, contrasted unfavorably with the log houses of their fellows at Gull Lake.

As we are on the trail of the Indian now, we might as well, for the edification of some of our friends, continue a brief space to discuss the untutored savage, his clothing, his customs, etc.:

Since the first days of his trading with the white man, the Indian has worn a blanket. It was the gift of the great Manitou to the poor Indian. It is his house, his home, his cover from the storm, his bed, his pillow, his delight. He clothes himself with it; he carries his children and burdens in it; he wraps it around him as a Roman toga. The blanket is the glory of the Indian, and it is a great shame if the government ever furnished him with shoddy, in place of the soft wool one he pays for, and to which he is entitled.

In addition to the blanket, the squaw usually stipulates for a dark blue broadcloth skirt and leggings to match. All Indians have small feet, protected by moccasins of buckskin. These smoke-dressed, hand-finished skins have no superior, if any equals, in the civilized markets; and the same, to my taste, may be said of the Indian maple sugar.

The age of any woman is always a delicate subject, but an Indian woman betrays her age at every step as she advances in life. You look for it not in her clouded face, nor in the wrinkles which seam it, but in the trail where she treads with her heavy burden. When young, her track is straight; when thirty, she begins to toe-in; and thereafter, as her burdens grow heavier, the angle of incidence increases. This sign also distinguishes the man from his mate, his feet turning neither to the right hand nor the left. It is one of the missions of Christianity to regulate the walk and the tracks of the red man, to lift the heavy burdens and bid the oppressed go free. This was the object of our great missionary to the Indians—to equalize the burdens of life, to raise woman to respectability, and make her a comrade for man, and, in her own sphere, ruler and queen.

Kahsahgah was the objective point towards which Dr. Breck was now concentrating all his energies. His attention had been directed to this large settlement of Indians (about 1,100) soon after his arrival at Gull Lake. Together with an officer of the Fort and the Rev. Solon W. Maney, chaplain of Fort Ripley at that time, he had made the journey by train, in the depths of winter when the mercury stood at eighteen degrees below. By train was the only means of travel in winter through this desolate wilderness. Between Gull Lake and Kahsahgah so obscure was the trail that but one Indian could be found to guide them. Of course, this was not a railroad train, but a long sort of toboggan, without runners, and a single horse or mule, with which the four, including the guide, made the journey in two days, camping out one night with only a blazing fire at their feet and a blanket stretched to shield their heads from the cutting winds of the north. One can fancy that only the fires of enthusiasm could have kept the blood circulating through such a night in the wilderness.

If anything I have written heretofore suggests small hardships and no dangers in the life of Dr. Breck, then I must hasten to assert that I have done the hero of my story great injustice. Dr. Breck seldom dwelt in his letters on the difficulties of the situation, and then in the most hopeful and cheerful spirit. He asked for no sympathy and desired no commiseration. Such souls scale the mountains as a roe. "They mount upon wings as eagles; they run, and are not weary; they walk, and are not faint." But still there were at times "hard trials and great tribulations." It might not be counted much to look steadily in the eye of a drunken savage whose club is raised to smite you down, and look and look until you have conquered the murderous spirit. Of course one could do it, but it would be a trial of nerve and will power not pleasant to exercise often. Dr. Brook had several victories of this sort to his credit at Kahsahgah.

I will say that Kahsahgah is the short for *Kah-sah-gahs-qua-gee-mo-kag*, and the eloquent chief of the same was "Flatmouth." I wish I knew his Indian, it might be an improvement on the translation.

## CHAPTER XXI

### TRAVELS AND DISCOVERIES

IN our last chapter we were considering some Indian traits and the position and characteristics of Lake Kahsahgah, where Dr. Breck was about to start his second mission among the Indians. This lake was sixty miles north of Kageash-koonsekog—or Gull Lake, as it is translated; between these lakes there was no direct communication until the government road was completed, and there were no Indians to be seen in all this distance. The average Indian is very provincial, and seldom wanders from his own immediate environment. It is a great occasion when he travels sixty miles from home. I presume the very opposite is the notion of the average white man who regards the original Indian as a wanderer, an Ishmaelite on the face of the earth. At the time, however, when Dr. Breck first visited Kahsahgah, there was but one Indian in all the large band of Pillager Indians located there—eleven hundred strong—who could be trusted as a guide between Kahsahgah and Gull Lake, although the distance was but sixty miles.

The conditions attending the founding of this new mission were altogether unlike, and much more favorable, than those connected with the beginnings of St. Columba, at Gull Lake. In the first instance Dr. Breck depended no longer entirely on himself and the resources he could create by his ready pen. In this last enterprise he was to receive large assistance from the general government. Although his first visit of exploration were attended by hardships and difficulties, his later ones were over a road which had cost the Indian Department the snug sum of $14,000. When Dr. Breck and family finally left St. Columba for Kahsahgah, they started at three o'clock in the morning and reached their destination at midnight of the same day, halting only to feed their horses and prepare a frugal meal for themselves. It must be understood that these horses were not ordinary nags, nor Indian ponies, but a fine span of horses, costing the government $400. This team the Indian Agent had presented to Dr. Breck some little time before he started this new mission. Before saying anything further of this second mission at Kahsahgah, it may be well to dispose of some matters connected with his prospecting journeys to other and more distant points. The accounts are brief, but sufficient to indicate the fact that Dr. Breck did not intend that any "pent-up Utica" should contract his powers, but evidently felt that the whole boundless regions of the Indian country were ours, if only we could manage to occupy and possess them.

In a letter dated January 16th, 1853, a year after Gull Lake was discovered by our little band, Dr. Breck writes to the Rev. Mr. Wilcoxson, from a distant point: "I have just returned from a trip to the most westerly bound of the Chippeways, 250 miles out by canoe. Brother Maney along; camping out every night." In these distant confines of the Chippeway nation they selected a site for another mission house upon the shores of one of the most beautiful lakes imaginable. They laid out extensive mission grounds, with the consent of the Indians, and staked out the position in a beautiful grove upon the finest table-land 100 feet above the water. They also laid out "a prairie farm of the best soil upon a stream that afforded a fine water power." How long these brave men were occupied in this work of preoccupation we are not informed. Just prior to this account, viz., June 13th, he writes of the same journey, and speaks particularly of the lake, the English of which is not given, and we only know it as the place of the date of his letter, but what after all is there in a name when it reads like this—June 13th, 1853, "Negigwaunowahsahgahigaw." "The scene before me," he says "is most beautiful; a lake fifteen or twenty miles in length, and five or eight in width. Perhaps not five white men have seen this lake, and to-morrow we may go where the white man has never been." You may wonder where this can be and what I am doing in these distant parts. I wonder at myself, but as the phrase runs, I am in for it, and therefore I stop at nothing. We have now accomplished about 250 miles, and the waters I have just described to you run into the Red River of Prince Rupert's Land. Indeed this lake is the head of that river," and he adds the interesting statement that "upon this lake lives the most westerly band of the Chippeway nations," and then follows this statement: "Beyond these Indians all is a waste and howling wilderness for three or four days' journey, and then you enter the country of the Sioux or Dakotas, the hereditary enemy of the Chippeways. It is a happy thought that providentially the distance was so great, as then the war trail would be longer, and the difficulties greater in the laudable effort to gather in from their enemies ponies and scalps, and other necessaries of life so esteemed by these untamed men of the wilderness." The leader and guides of Drs. Breck and Maney in these expeditions, including a trip to Otter Tail Lake, was an African Ojibway by the name of George Bungo, a well educated descendent of a negro, kidnapped by the Chippeways in 1878, and brought from Chicago to the St. Croix River. Dr. Breck says that he was coal black, a large, fine-looking man, enjoying the confidence of all who knew him. His wife was an Ojibway woman, but his children were of a light complexion and very finely featured. It seems to have been at the solicitation of this respectable man that Dr. Breck came to visit that distant point. Doubtless Mr. Bungo had in view also the future education of these same handsome—let us say, as we may in our ignorance, daughters. There were beside Mr. Bungo, also two Canadian French half-breeds to aid in propelling the canoe. Having now cleared away the side issues we shall in our next look after the new mission located at Kahsahgah.

## CHAPTER XXII

### THE INTELLIGENCE OF THE INDIAN

As some people are disposed to be incredulous when we speak of the intelligence of the Indian and his appreciation of the blessings of a Christian civilization, we quote the following letter to Dr. Breck from the old chief, Flatmouth, who was at the head of this large band of Indians at Kahsahgah. It was written long before it was even proposed to establish the new mission; indeed, within a year, I think, after Dr. Breck had begun his work at Gull Lake.

"My friend, since I saw you, you have always been in my memory. I have since thought of a great many things you could do to better our condition. My friend, you cannot imagine how anxious I am to have you come and live among us, and oh, how glad I will be when I come home from my hunt and see some part of your house put up on the border of our lake. This lake has been owned by my forefathers, and no one will have a word to say when I have made my promises. I now say to you, come and choose out a place which is not occupied anywhere about our lake, and take and use freely anything, wood, hay, fish, etc., which will make your comfortable. My friend, I shall leave in a few days for my hunt, and shall not be back again before the spring opens. My friend, if you have any compassion for us and our children, you will not hesitate, and come now and choose a place for your home. I shall leave word with Buffalo and the old men what to say to you. They will not be bad words, but good ones, that they will speak. My friend, when I get back from my hunt and see you getting ready to live among us, I will then be glad to know that some of our people will have the opportunity to learn from whence the whites get their knowledge. My friend, this is all at present, and I hope the Great Spirit will spare my life until I see you living among us."

It was this letter which suggested and compelled Dr. Breck's attention to Kah-sah-gah-squa-jeo-ma-kag. But now that the time had fully arrived when Dr. Breck must give up St. Columba into other hands, many perplexing questions had to be settled. Could he undertake to raise funds for both? Could he find the right man to supply his place at St. Columba? Hitherto on all important questions he had consulted good and wise Bishop Kemper, and now once more he seeks his counsel and advice. First, he suggests himself that it would be the right and proper thing that the domestic committee should take St. Columba off his hands entirely, and thus set him free to begin the new mission untrammeled

by other responsibilities, but this would involve
a large expenditure of money, and so the Board
did not approve, and would only consent to pay
a missionary stipend to some clergyman whom
Dr. Breck might select. This, Dr. Breck thought,
indicated a very poor appreciation of the value
of the work already accomplished, to say nothing
of the future prospects of usefulness for the mission.
He was disappointed and indignant at
what he regarded as a wholesale lack of faith. If
they could spare $18,000 a year for office expenses,
he thought they could afford to be more liberal to
the only mission of our Church among the Indians
of the far West. To the Board, then, it
certainly must have seemed the day of very small
things for Indian missions. Dr. Breck's response
to this indicates his own courage and resourcefulness:
"If the Board is distrustful and timid,
I will assume all responsibilities. I will raise the
money and run both missions myself." But if
the Bishop could secure no relief in this direction,
he fortunately was able to name the man
who would "fill the bill" as a substitute. He
was certain the Rev. E. Steele Peake, B. D., and
his excellent wife were the very ones to carry on
the work. Of Mr. Peake, an early graduate
of Nashotah, we have already spoken as one
of the providential men raised up for this very
work and time, and so we find that Mr.
Peake and his wife arrived at St. Columba
the very day that Dr. Breck and family left

with their fine team over the new government road for Kahsahgah.

The journey was a sort of "forced march" of over sixty miles along a single track. Through extensive forests and round lakes of the clearest water, they saw no human habitation, and they met no man in all the long day of their lonely journey—until nine o'clock in the evening, when they enjoyed a veritable surprise. The surprise was first and the enjoyment afterwards, as we may well imagine. Says Dr. Breck: "One scene in the deep, dark woods occurred that might have affrighted stouter hearts than ours. It was near midnight and almost impenetrable forests lay on either side of us. While pursuing our journey alone through these woods, suddenly we heard whoops and yells answering one another. They were evidently coming nearer to us. The red man over the hills had heard the rumbling of the white man's wheels over the frozen earth. There was no turning aside, had we been disposed to avoid the meeting. But I had learned the Indian better than some that were with me, and we pursued our way as though nothing strange were happening. Within half a mile we saw lights in the distance. As we approached nearer the shouting ceased and birch-bark torches appeared ahead on either side of the narrow track. Soon wigwams were seen on both sides of the road and a large company of chiefs, braves and women with their children and pappooses, thronged us.

We now stopped and saluted them." These Indians were a part of the Pillager Band doubtless on their way to receive their annual payment, and they availed themselves of this circumstance to extend an earnest welcome to the missionary.

Dr. Breck's Indian name was Mak-uhd-ay-akuh-naya, perhaps Mak for short, or when, as we say, time was money. Translated, it is "Black Robe," or "Man in the Cassock." The name for bishop needs no translation, but is sufficient in itself for all ordinary occasions, and runs thusly, "Ne-he-shi-ma-kuh-da-ya-kuh-na-ya-me-ne-mah-neg." It is singular, but a fact, that an Indian boy will shuffle off these long names in such glib fashion that you would suppose it no more of a name than Tom Jones or Johnson.

## CHAPTER XXIII

#### THE NEW MISSION

THE site chosen by Dr. Breck on Lake Kahsahgah for his new mission was very striking. It was a high promontory extending into the lake. Like the city set upon the hill it could not be hid. Indeed, it was visible from almost every part of the lake—reminding one of the fact that Nashotah and Faribault, and St. Columba, and Benicia, not to mention St. Paul, were all of them selected by one who possessed a rare sense of the appropriate, and who felt that "a thing of beauty was a joy forever."

In order to understand that which characteristically distinguished the new enterprise at Kahsahgah, he must bear in mind that for the first and last time in the history of his life-work Dr. Breck was not alone in his responsibilities. Through the influence of the Hon. Henry M. Rice, congressman from the new territory of Minnesota, the Indian Department had committed to Dr. Breck the educating and civilizing of the Chippeway nation—or, as Dr. Breck expresses it: "The general Government has offered to my acceptance the school and civilization fund for these Indians." Then he goes on to explain as follows: "The buildings for the school are to be put up at the expense of the Government; we are limited to a certain amount a year for these buildings, as well as for the support of the children who are to be received into them. I am left to my own judgment as regards these buildings, what they are to be, etc. Three laborers are given into my charge, selected by myself, and paid by the Government. Besides, 200 acres of land are to be cleared, and plowed at the expense of the Government, and this work is also in my hands to oversee. Indians are recommended to be employed for all work when they can be induced to labor." This was to be done outside all other allowances, and Dr. Breck was to be responsible to the Indian agent for all, except the method of carrying on the work.

Dr. Breck fully realized that to Christianize the Indian, he must first be civilized. He says also: "I have selected a bold shore and a beautiful sugar grove for our mission," and now in the midst of his felicitations, he adds, what he could never have said before in any similar enterprise, "I am also happy in having a wife who is glad to go with me into this wilderness for the love she also has for this Indian work." There was also in Dr. Breck's family at this time Mr. Parker and wife and one child, and also the son and heir—the consolation and hope of his father's heart, William Augustus Muhlenberg Breck, then but a few months old—now in the ministry of the Church, and assistant of Holy Trinity, San Francisco. Then there was the mission farmer, Mr. Reese, and his wife and five children. In addition to this family there were ladies, and Indian children—sixteen of them—who were sheltered and fed and taught, all under the roof of the first buildings erected by the Government for this object.

This was the condition existing three months after Dr. Breck had given up St. Columba to the care and supervision of his successor, the Rev. Mr. Peake. It was about this time that Bishop Kemper paid his first and only visit to this distant region of the Northwest. It was the intention that he should visit both St. Columba and Kahsahgah for Confirmations and that he might see with his own eyes—now growing dim with advancing years—the noble work of which he had so often heard, and in which from the first he had taken an absorbing interest. We can well imagine the joy of the meeting between these two great missionaries, the Bishop of unceasing labors and endless jurisdiction, and the man who had outstripped all other men of his day and generation in the planting of the banner of the Church, even beyond all the outposts of civilization. The Bishop did indeed reach St. Columba, where he spent a week enjoying one of his longest rests. A large class of candidates was presented for the "Laying on of hands," truly apostolic, but the inclemency of the season forbade his intended journey to Kahsahgah, greatly to his disappointment. After many interesting services the Bishop returned to St. Paul and Dr. Breck to Kahsahgah to urge on the great work which seemed to be only awaiting the husbandman in order soon to reap a golden harvest.

At this moment Dr. Breck was at the very summit of his ambitions so far as this Indian work was ever destined to attain. Like Moses, he also beheld the promised land; he saw as in a vision from his vantage ground at Kahsahgah all the Indian country covered with churches and missions, and all the Indians themselves clothed, and in their right minds, sitting at the feet of Christian teachers, a diocese organized with its presbyters and its Bishop. Alas! that such hopes and dreams must perish, as in a night. What prophet could then have foretold the morrow? What seer have surmised the wrack and ruin that was to follow a morning so bright with the promise of a serene and cloudless day? Scarcely had the mission got under way before mutterings of the storm were heard. Strong hearts were dismayed. Life even was in jeopardy and flight the only alternative left for those who would escape the fury of a nation of savages, mad and wild and drunk until there was not one left sober to tell the story of their shame and their degradation.

## CHAPTER XXIV

### THE NEW MISSION—CONTINUED

For six months all went prosperously for the Kahsahgah mission. The foundation of the Church of the Good Shepherd had been laid and the funds were promised to complete the building, which moneys afterwards were transferred, with the consent of the donor, Miss Edwards, to Faribault, and employed in the erection of the church of the same title there. When Dr. Breck reached Kahsahgah with his family in the fall of 1856, the young men and Chief Flatmouth himself, had already departed to their winter hunting-ground, from which they did not return until the following spring. It was their custom to come back in time for sugar-making in March and April. Jerked venison, pelts, and maple sugar *plus* the annual payments from the Government, was the source from which their revenues of money were derived. Dr. Breck was therefore left in peace during the winter. But when the Indians returned from their hunt, then troubles began.

As there were no troops to police the country, whiskey entered from every side, and although it was unlawful to sell liquor to the Indians, yet in the village of Crow-wing alone, seven saloons

## The New Mission—Continued

"distilled the deadly dew," and soon the entire country was flooded with the intoxicating beverage, and every Indian with plenty of money soon found himself drunk "as a lord" and ready for any act of violence. Not less than four hundred Indians were reported drunk at one time at Kahsahgah. I quote here largely from the letters of Dr. Breck to Bishop Kemper and other friends of the mission:

"The past six weeks at Leech Lake (Kahsahgah) has been a dearly bought experience with our mission. The drunken Indian has visited us at our mission house at various times. My own experience has been to be kept at bay in Mrs. Breck's private room by the drawn knife of the half-drunken savage. On another occasion a large dark Indian danced like a maniac in the midst of the broken glass of our front windows which were smashed to atoms by himself and others. I went out to them by a back door, but upon my following a white man who was pursued by an Indian, this man at the window demanded my life, and only by art and with great difficulty was he kept from bursting open Mrs. Breck's door with a great club. The next day this hideous monster said to one of our men that I had escaped this time, but the next he would have me."

These scenes were of almost daily occurrence, and the chiefs who were friendly declared they were unable to afford any protection. Dr. Breck goes on to say: "The above violence took place some time since but in different forms, and finally in one more aggravated than all the rest. We have been brought to a standpoint, so that we must leave, as we have no other resource left—we must either resort to arms or perish. I have never turned my back upon the plow I have taken hold of, neither do I now, but I see no martyrdom in laying down life for drunkenness, and this result—the death of some of us—is certain where there is no law in the nation, or over the nation. If we take the sword may we not perish with the sword as many brave soldiers, and lately (in March last) forty settlers have at the hands of the Sioux. These Indians during drunkenness habitually fight one another, and many have been killed and many wounded during their affrays in the last two years. P. S.—I have brought the entire mission family away. Part of the Indian children (of the household) I have left at St. Columba, and part of the laborers are there also." "I should have added," he concludes, "that one of the female and one male teacher also were struck by drunken Indians. The former was so injured and frightened that she dismissed her school and took to her bed. This was Miss West." The above is dated Fort Ripley, where the fleeing missionaries had taken refuge.

The entire time spent by Dr. Breck and his family at Kahsahgah was eight months, viz., from November 12th, 1856 to July 16th, 1857.

It was in this interval that the secretary of war, General Floyd, of confederate fame, removed all the troops south from this section of the Northwest. This dastardly act naturally exposed the frontier settlers to an uprising of the Indians, which actually took place farther south among the Sioux, and resulted in the massacre of a great number of border people.

The mission at St. Columba was at this period in charge of the Rev. Mr. Peake who, with his good wife and Enmegabowh (deacon), held possession for several years after Dr. Breck had left the Indian country. But matters did not improve among the Indians as time passed, and the disturbances were of so fearful a character that Mr. Peake was constrained to remove from St. Columba to Crow-wing, on the river, and but seven miles above Fort Ripley. St. Columba was supplied with services from our Indian deacon, Enmegabowh, Mr. Peake, meanwhile, going out once a month to administer the Holy Eucharist. In order to relieve Dr. Breck of his support, Mr. Peake became at Crow-wing a missionary of the Domestic Board, to which he made report of his work among the white settlers, while he still gave account to Dr. Breck, at Faribault, of the condition of the Indian field.

Dr. Breck was desirous at this time of turning over all his correspondence relating to the Indians to Mr. Peake, but this was declined through the advice of wise Bishop Kemper, so that Dr. Breck all through—until relieved by Bishop Whipple—was responsible as the head of the Associate Mission for the Indians.

It is, of course, impossible at this late day to realize the frightful condition of the Indian field at that period. I am confident that nothing short of the most deadly danger to all concerned would have forced Dr. Breck to abandon Kahsahgah at its most hopeful moment. Indeed he regarded his leaving but as a temporary suspension of the work so auspiciously begun, but it is the marvel of the man that no sooner was he persuaded that it was all up with the Kahsahgah mission, than with the most sublime confidence he turned his attention and his energies to the new field and the new work which loomed up before his imagination at Faribault. The courage and the resourcefulness of the man soon blazed out another path for his untiring feet —feet that never flagged—nor grew weary until he sank to rest on the shores of the western ocean.

## CHAPTER XXV

### "WARS AND RUMORS OF WARS"

On his return to St. Paul, Dr. Breck at once undertook the new work at Faribault. He always found in defeat the stepping stone to a new enterprise. He was as full of resources as a great general on the field of battle—when he resigned the presidency at Nashotah he made ready to start for St. Paul; when blocked in his design to establish a theological school at St. Paul, he was off at once for the Indian field; when driven back and out of the Indian field, he immediately organized the Associate Mission and began laying his foundations at Faribault. He lost no time in idle regrets—his lips uttered no complaints; he simply accepted the situation, and with sublime faith and a courage wonderful to behold, entered upon the new field. Like the great Frederick, he never knew when he was beaten, and in this sublime ignorance he turned disaster into success, and won victories where other men had abandoned the field in despair. It was but a short time after he reached St. Paul that his home fires were burning at Faribault, and his Indian children were gathered about him, and there for a time we will leave him, while we return to St. Columba and the little flock left in the wilderness during all these unhappy years between 1857 and 1862.[1]

The Rev. Mr. Peake and Enmegahbowh had been left in charge of the well-equipped mission of St. Columba, at Gull Lake. Dr. Breck, on his retreat from Kahsahgah, in July, 1857, stayed but half a day at St. Columba. There was no reason for his remaining longer, for the work there was already in competent hands. Mr. Peake remained in charge of St. Columba and its school for three years, Enmegahbowh having, meanwhile, been ordained to the diaconate by Bishop Kemper, at Faribault. Upon his return to St. Columba, he was put in charge of the mission, and moved his family into the Mission House, Mr. Peake taking his family to Crow Wing and becoming a missionary of the General Board to the whites; this change having become a necessity by reason of the lack of funds to support longer two men in the Indian field. Crow Wing is situated, as is Fort Ripley, on the Mississippi River. To reach Gull Lake from the fort, you go up the river seven miles to Crow Wing, from there you cross the river and travel west twelve miles into the country, when you find yourself at the Gull Lake mission. To understand what follows in the history of St. Columba, it is important that one have an idea of the lay of the land, and the relative locations

[1] See "Note on Faribault," on page 193.

of these several points. It is well to mention the fact here that the reservation at White Earth had already been set apart for the Indians, and, therefore, the country outside that hundred miles square was now open to white settlers, and, as usual, they were not slow to avail themselves of this privilege. The Indians still roamed at large, and it was not until after the outbreak in 1862 that they were obliged to live on the reservation, so that the whites and Indians were very much mixed up in those prehistoric days; and when the soldiers were withdrawn from Fort Ripley, and the Indians were free of fear, it is no wonder that confusion and chaos reigned in all the region round about.

In 1858 matters reached such a dangerous state that Governor Medaver, of Minnesota, prevailed on the general government to send soldiers back to keep the peace and protect white families from injury. Then for a short time the land had rest; but only for a brief space, for the soldiers were again sent away, and all hearts quaked with fear, not knowing how soon the general outbreak would come. The condition was so threatening in the fall of 1858, that the Rev. Mr. Peake was constrained to move his whole household to the fort, where he had quarters assigned him, and where for a good part of the winter he carried on his Indian school. When times became more quiet, he returned again to St. Columba. The withdrawal of the soldiers before the opening of our great Civil War was the beginning of Secretary Floyd's policy to dismantle all the forts along our Northern frontier. How shall we characterize such conduct when we know that the removal of these soldiers exposed all the border people—men, women, and children—to the tomahawk and scalping knife of the savages? In 1857, the Sioux surprised and massacred twenty-seven white people at Springfield, Iowa, and carried off four white women into a hideous captivity. "Soldiers all gone; white man must look out," said a representative Indian. Such was the condition in 1862.

# CHAPTER XXVI

## ENMEGAHBOWH AND THE INDIAN WAR

WHEN I spoke of the providential man, Enmegahbowh, who first suggested the Indian mission to Dr. Breck, I did not then know that he was also the saviour of the work at St. Columba, and of that whole country, from a great Indian war in 1863.

The Sioux, under the leadership of Little Crow, were already on the warpath farther to the south. The soldiers had been removed from Fort Ripley, and the entire country was in the first throes of the great Civil War, so that the occasion was ripe for the Chippeways to rise and avenge their old wrongs at the hands of the whites. To precipitate the outbreak, for which everything was favorable, Little Crow sent a deputation to Pok-o-nak-e-shik—or Hole-in-the-day—the war chief of the Chippeways, inviting his cooperation in a general massacre of all the border settlers. After a council had been summoned, and a delay of a few days, the deputation was dismissed to Little Crow, with the assurance that he—Hole-in-the-day—would join with him in his war on the whites. This conspiracy was kept a profound secret, and only came to the knowledge of Enmegahbowh at Gull Lake by what seemed a special providence, and at the last moment when it could have become known with any profit to the doomed village of Crow Wing. Hole-in-the-day summoned his braves far and near, and three hundred responded at once. It soon became known to many of the white people that a large band of Indians was encamped in the neighborhood, but they did not dare to flee because the Indians had policed the country, and a man hazarded his life if caught away from home.

Enmegahbowh was practically a prisoner in the Mission House at St. Columba. One day, to his astonishment, he saw these three hundred Indians pass near the mission in single file with war paint and armed as if for battle, but what the meaning of it all was, he could only surmise. He knew there was mischief brewing, but what form it would assume, he did not know until the Thursday night before the Sunday on which the massacre of the entire village, men, women and children, had been determined. About ten o'clock at night, a friendly chief—Crossing Sky—entered the Mission House and informed Enmegahbowh and his faithful wife, Re-wah-bik-ke-shigs Equa, that Crow Wing was to be surprised the next Sunday morning before daybreak; on Saturday all the Indians would leave Gull Lake to be ready for the battle, and so it would be possible, then, to escape in a canoe to the fort, by way of the lake and Gull River, which enters the Mississippi near and a little below the village of Crow Wing. It is at this point that the brave wife's voice is heard urging that some one must warn the villagers, and that either she or Enmegahbowh must go at all risks; but as her husband was closely watched, she knew he would never reach the village alive, and so she would undertake the twelve-mile night journey alone; but this was not to be; for just then the door opened, and in slipped another scared man, by the name of Yorknight. "What is all this drumming and war whoops about?" said he, and Enmegahbowh replied: "Sunday morning next, all these warriors will attack your village; you must go and warn them and take a letter from me." When the man trembled and said, "I cannot go, they will kill me," Enmegahbowh replied: "You go, or I or my wife must go." This closed the discussion, and the man went his way. Saturday the hostile Indians left Gull Lake, and in the same night, about ten o'clock, Enmegahbowh, his wife, and children, embarked in a birch canoe, and reached the fort in safety about ten o'clock the next day.

Enmegahbowh was received by the only officer left at the fort with great joy, as there were no soldiers to defend the fort, and at his urgent request, Enmegahbowh shouldered a musket, and acted as sentinel all that day and the night following. No one as yet knew what had befallen at Crow Wing, and they were in great distress and fear, for if the Indians were successful there, the mad savages would at once attack and capture the fort. Here I quote from the letter of Enmegahbowh: "Towards evening, Sunday, the joyous news was brought in to the effect that the warriors had failed to make an attack on the village. When the Indians arrived a quarter of a mile from the village they had sent out two spies to see if any preparations had been made for defense. When these arrived at the village they found that a strong stockade had been erected, which it would be very difficult to attack successfully; this they reported to Hole-in-the-day who was exceedingly angry, and said he knew who the traitor was, and he would kill him on sight."

The messenger sent by Enmegahbowh had, it seems, arrived safe and sound at Crow Wing, and had delivered the letter, which advised that a strong stockade should be built, and so all the people worked day and night to complete it in time. Had this first attempt succeeded, the Indians, intoxicated with blood and murder, would have taken the fort, and all the whites of that region would have been the victims of the tomahawk and scalping knife. The insurrection ended where it began. Hole-in-the-day dismissed his warriors, and Enmegahbowh shortly returned to the Mission House at St. Columba.

For his eminent services in this matter Enmegahbowh was recompensed by the government by a grant of 360 acres of land. The threat of

Hole-in-the-day to kill Enmegahbowh he tried to carry out by shortly sending to the Mission House two Indians to murder him. They arrived about nine o'clock in the morning, but Johnson had been warned, and although his conscience did not permit him to handle firearms, he stretched a point, and loaded his double-barrel gun, and gave it to his wife who was known as a good shot, and who had asked him to let her take the matter into her own hands. As the savages approached, she threw open the door, and shouted: "I know what you have come for, but the first one who shows a weapon, I will shoot down like a dog." They knew her reputation as a woman of spirit, and skill with the gun, and at once abandoned their design, and made her a present. These same Indians confessed they had been sent by Hole-in-the-day, and acknowledged that Enmegahbowh had not only saved the whites, but the Indians also from being all destroyed by the government, so there was cause for mutual congratulations. Afterwards, as indicating their love and respect for Enmegahbowh, when all the Indians were removed to White Earth, over one hundred of the chiefs and principal men sent a petition asking him to come and live with them at White Earth, promising to become Christians and do what he advised for their good, and there he went, their pastor and friend, full of honors and years, waiting in meekness and patience for the summons of his beloved Master, whom through a long and eventful life he has served faithfully and efficiently.

The church at St. Columba was destroyed, some say, by white men. Mr. Peake served as chaplain in our Civil War three years, and then became chaplain of St. Mary's School, Faribault.

## CHAPTER XXVII

### SIOUX AND OJIBWAYS

In a former chapter, we indicated that Dr. Breck had settled upon Faribault as the home of the Associate Mission, consisting of himself, Rev. Mr. Maney, and the Rev. Mr. Peake. Dr. Breck had brought with him from Kahsahgah and St. Columba about twenty Indian adults and children. These were under the supervision of Mrs. Breck,—who had proven herself an earnest and efficient helper in the work of Indian missions, so that from the first there was the nucleus of an educational institution soon to develop into schools for boys and girls, and eventually to include a theological department for the education and training of young men for the work of the ministry.

I am very desirous to impress upon the minds of my readers the fact that Dr. Breck was at this point entering upon the last half of his life work, and that this part was just as remarkable as that which went before. Dr. Breck, from the first, had it in mind to lay foundations in Minnesota for church schools at the same time that he was planting missions and doing the work of a pastor and evangelist. When after two years' labor at St. Paul he found he could not secure the consent of Bishop Kemper to carry out his heart's desire, the opportunity to interest himself for the Indians suddenly appeared—"A door was opened"—and a hand beckoned him to enter upon a new and strange experience. This Indian work, in after years, seemed almost a side issue undertaken to fill up the time of preparation for the greatest achievement of his wonderful life, the founding of Faribault, and yet at the time the good man believed that the Indian field was to be the scene of all his future work. Never did it appear more true than now, that while "Man proposes, God disposes." The Indian work was indeed most important,—at this particular juncture, as a preparation for the burying of the hatchet between the two most powerful of all the Indian tribes upon this continent. When I went to St. Paul in 1850, the Sioux of the south and the plains, and the Ojibways of the north and the woods, were at war, as they had been from time immemorial. Gradually the former had given way before their enemies, until they had been driven west and south of the Mississippi River. Sometimes a Sioux Indian would cross the river to trade, but he was very careful to encounter no Ojibways in the streets of St. Paul. Dr. Breck's mission among the Ojibways and afterwards his Faribault mission fifty miles west and south of the river in Sioux territory, was largely the means of destroying the enmity existing between these hostile tribes.

At this time the two nations were almost equal in strength, numbering each about 20,000 souls, and if the Indian mission had only accomplished this one thing—of promoting peace, the venture had wrought a world of good,—and another thought not less important, is that a great Indian massacre was averted through the courage and foresight of our Indian missionary at St. Columba, as we have described it in a recent chapter.

God's ways are indeed inscrutable. We read of famous Indian treaties, and important councils held, since the days of William Penn, but where will you find greater results than the actual destruction of the enmity existing between two great nations of savages, and the averting of a hideous border war at a time when all the troops had been removed to distant parts of the country, to say nothing of the actual results in the Christianizing of many pagan people, which became the real initiative of all the Indian work of our church, and which is now manifest, as in the Diocese of Niobrara and other fields, where flourish many Indian schools and churches. Bishop Whipple has been called the "Apostle of the Indians," and he has proved under obloquy and abuse, that he deserved the title and the praise which has followed his vindication; but after all that is or can be said, he and others builded on that foundation which was laid in the peace secured between Chippeway and Sioux as one of the results of the mission at St. Columba.

## CHAPTER XXVIII

### FARIBAULT

It is not to be understood that all the Indian work at St. Columba had been swept away at the time Dr. Breck fled with his wife and Indian family from Kahsahgah. The mission buildings at St. Columba were indeed partially destroyed, and Enmegahbowh and his family were obliged to seek safety within the defenses of Fort Ripley, —but the mission was shortly occupied again by the missionary, and the work went on as before. Afterwards the Indians were removed to the White Earth Reservation, and from that day to the time of his death, Enmegahbowh ministered to their spiritual needs.

Bishop Whipple was consecrated in 1859, and at once visited all the Indian fields,—opening new stations and strengthening the "things that remained,"—but all these splendid results had their initiative in the Mother Mission at St. Columba.

Having said this much to fully clear the way, we return to the new field at Faribault, where we find a population of a few hundred people and three communicants, as the "mustard seed" of the new enterprise. A clean slate, however, was all that Dr. Breck required—he preferred to lay his own foundations—and to build up the congregation while erecting the church. First he opened a school for his Indian refugees, and in this schoolroom he held daily and Sunday services. It is safe to say that he visited every house in the village within the first two months, by the end of which time he and his associates held services in every new settlement within a radius of twenty-five miles. Wherever he found children or adults unbaptized, he at once began their preparation for baptism or confirmation. He literally visited from house to house. It was his idea of an "Associate Mission"—that the clergy who composed it should cover all points within a day's journey from the centre of operations,—that in the course of their travels they should stop at every house and ascertain if any had church affiliations. Now and then they discovered a family long deprived of church ordinances, and in several instances entire households were baptized. Dr. Breck's missions were all "Associate Missions"—and wherever the central station was located, schools were opened for boys and girls, with the idea of eventually forming strong educational institutions, which, in time, should furnish young men for the ministry,—and Christian mothers for generations yet unborn. On the foundations laid by Dr. Breck at Faribault, have been erected the splendid schools of Bishop Whipple, which are to-day the glory of the church in all the great Northwest. St. Mary's school for girls, and Shattuck school for boys, and the Seabury Divinity Hall,—speak eloquently the wisdom of their founder, who for nine years in season and out of season labored for their upbuilding,—and only left them when assured of their future, and when he felt himself called upon to turn his face " westward where the course of empire takes its way."

While at Faribault two sore trials befell Dr. Breck,—one was the loss of his wife (*nee* Miss Mills), and the other the loss by fire of all his household effects,—including his precious library, and even the traditional " barrel " of sermons perished. All these children of his brain went up in flame except the last leaf of a single sermon, on which was written: " These men were steadfast to their profession of the true God in the midst of the burning fiery furnace." The significant comment of Dr. Breck upon his losses was the half humorous remark,—" I should think it a good time for me to emigrate to the West." At this period, 1869, all his schools were flourishing; Bishop Whipple had finally settled the long vexed question of the Episcopal residence at Faribault, for which St. Paul had contended from the first, on account of its being the chief city of the state, and principally because the original purchase of seven acres of ground in the centre of the city afforded abundant room for a cathedral-church, and the schools and hospitals which go to make up a complete ecclesiastical establishment. But Providence ordered that Faribault, and not St. Paul, should become the Bishop's choice. One of the last acts of Dr. Breck before leaving Faribault for the far Pacific coast was the additional purchase of twenty acres of land to enlarge the church's freehold, at a cost of $2,000. The value of church property in the Diocese when Dr. Breck left Minnesota, approximated $100,000. In 1894 the secretary of the Board remarked, "it is a safe estimate to say that the property of the Board, including the Endowment Fund Building, and certificates of deposit is now worth over $80,000, and it owes no man anything except its debt of gratitude to its founders." From the Breck investments in real estate the report reads: "From annual income, paid by the treasurer of the Episcopate Fund for the support of the Bishop of the Diocese from January 1, 1867, to June 1, 1893, $33,057.82, a total capital and product of $123,057.82. The value of Faribault real estate, not including buildings was near or quite $30,000, —and if the church's real estate in 1868, when Dr. Breck left it, was so much, then with the buildings erected since by Bishop Whipple at Faribault for his schools, the diocesan property to-day must have a value of at least $500,000. I have thought this financial side-light upon the layer of foundations, would give some idea of Dr. Breck's character as a financier, and help to a correct estimate of his services to the church in

Minnesota,—and in this connection we are not to overlook the 465 acres of land he purchased in 1843, as a future endowment for Nashotah. He was indeed a master builder, 'who builded even better than he knew.'"

Dr. Breck did not work for wages, nor seek in real estate a fortune for himself. Just before leaving Minnesota he says: "Although a missionary for a quarter of a century, and already feeling the sure signs of age creeping on, I have never thought of self when making rich gain in lands and houses for the church, for I shall go forth from this whole work with hands clean from all contact with worldly possessions—even to an acre of land, or so much as the nail of a dwelling."

## CHAPTER XXIX

### THE HALL OF FAME

The men who lay foundations to endure are always strong men. The Church in Minnesota has ever been distinguished for the character of its churchmanship,—for its loyalty, for its aggressive and yet conservative spirit. But this could not have been except its foundations had been strongly laid. Fortunately then there were no such names as, "High, Low, Broad," to distract the sinner who sought the Saviour. There was but one mind and one heart. There was an honest acceptance of the Church as a body, "which was wiser than her wisest member, and holier than her holiest member." Between 1850 and 1860 the population of the State increased with astonishing rapidity. In that period all the present towns on the river sprang into existence, strong parishes were built up, as at St. Paul, Minneapolis, Winona, Faribault and Red Wing. I speak now only of this first decade. In this period the foundations were all laid of the first work of the Church in Minnesota, and singularly by twelve apostolic men, all of whom deserve a place in this "Hall of Fame."

There were first the two men who were the

official leaders, Bishops Kemper and Whipple, "whose fame is in all the Churches"; we can therefore leave them here at the head of the line, and go on to the parish and missionary clergy who opened the way, and who built up the churches and congregations, on the one foundation, "which is, Jesus Christ, the Lord."

There was Dr. Geer, the sturdy Chaplain at Fort Snelling,—who was full of missionary zeal and enthusiasm. He held the first services in St. Paul. Then following came Dr. Breck and his associates, Wilcoxson and Merrick, whom we need only to mention here.

The Rev. John Van Ingen, D. D., Rector of Christ Church, St. Paul, and founder of the Church Hospital in that city. The good doctor opened his own house for a hospital, even when there was difficulty in discovering the first patient. I always loved to hear him preach; once he illustrated the importance of religion, by saying, "That all our expenses were for either luxuries, comforts or necessities. If your religion is a luxury, you will cut it off with these luxuries first, if it is a comfort only, then it goes with your comforts, but if it a necessity then you will divide with it your last crust. Judge yourselves, brethren; is your religion a luxury, a comfort or is it a necessity?"

Dr. Paterson, a man of wealth, with a most charming family, invested in real estate, in St. Paul. He built St. Paul's Church in the lower town and soon had a large and influential congregation. Dr. Paterson was a strong candidate for the first Episcopate and it was he who nominated Henry B. Whipple, of Chicago, who was elected on the second ballot, a sudden and unexpected ending of a strong contest. "It was the unexpected that happened"—in this instance to the enduring disgust of the parties concerned in the result, but a wise choice as all the world is witness to-day.

Dr. S. Y. McMasters, Rector of Christ Church, St. Paul, was one of the strong men of the West at that time. He was a moderate Churchman, a literary man, interested greatly in the sciences, and the humanities, a staunch friend, of rugged mould, but like Dr. Geer, of a tender heart. I lay at his feet this tribute of personal regard and loving memory. There was at that period also the perpetual missionary, Mr. Chamberlain, son-in-law of Philander Chase—the first Bishop of Illinois. He was never a rector in all his long ministry, so he willed it. He was a very striking personality, with long black hair, deep set eyes and a voice like a bassoon. It was reported that he had fourteen mission stations under his care and had built a Gothic Church at every station. Whipple and Breck and Wilcoxson and Chamberlain and Van Ingen were all men of statue and averaged over six feet in height. To these names in our "Hall of Fame" we must add the name of Edward Randolph Welles, the first Rector of

Christ Church, Red Wing. He was elected to the Episcopate of Wisconsin in 1874. This parish was founded by two laymen, Dr. Hawley and Judge Wilder. A legend of the former is interesting. Red Wing has a picturesque site on the Mississippi just above Lake Pepin and was early peopled by the Methodists, who dearly love their own and isolation, as at Evanston, Ill., and Ocean Grove, N. J.; so exclusive was their spirit that when Dr. Hawley thought to locate there, he was informed that none but a Methodist physician would be tolerated or could prosper in that lovely spot. The temper of the young doctor would none of this. He declared to the delegation sent to wait upon him, that if such was the state of things he would certainly remain—that he was a Churchman and an American. "I will," he declared, "remain, and I will show you that in two years we will build right here in Red Wing, 'a Church of the Living God.'" This parish was self-supporting from the first and now with a communicant list of 426 persons, flourishes as one of the banner parishes of the State.

When Dr. Breck left Faribault for California, the Rev. Elisha P. Thomas, D. D., had become secretary of the Associate Mission at Faribault. He afterwards built St. Mark's Church, Minneapolis. Then he was rector of St. Paul's Church, St. Paul, from which position he was elected Bishop of Kansas. Metaphysics and the sciences interested him. He was very successful as a financier and raised large sums for the Diocese. He was also at one time Professor of Hebrew at Faribault.

Of the Rev. E. Steele Peake we have already spoken. He was the one man from Nashotah who stood with Dr. Breck in the Indian missions.

At this moment and while I write comes the sad news of the passing of "Enmegahbowh," the man who "opened the door" to the Indian field, who was first an interpreter then a priest of the Church. At the extreme age of ninety-three years he finds his rest and reward. This man who came from the wilds of paganism, was an honor to the Church he so faithfully served. His one great disappointment in life was the early death of his boy, Alfred, at the age of twelve years, a lad of unusual promise, and good and wise beyond his years. Just before his death he declared his readiness to go, and comforted all his friends by his cheerful words of love and hope. He took his father's hand at last and with earnest look said, "Father, pray much and do good"; this was the motto of his own daily Christian life and might well entitle him to be mentioned together with his father in this chapter of worthies.

The Rev. Solon W. Maney, at first Chaplain and then Professor at Faribault, is certainly entitled to a place in our "Hall of Fame." He was short and round and jolly, the life and hope that cheered every company; a wise and able instructor, a good preacher, and full of missionary enthusiasm. He too was one of the originals.

The Rev. David Buel Knickerbocker was perhaps the strongest personality, and the most effective worker in the new Diocese. He started Gethseminary Parish, the mother of all the fourteen churches of Minneapolis. The first convention of the Diocese with its new Bishop was held in his church at which the writer was present. This parish is one of the largest in the west, having 1,267 communicants. Dr. Knickerbocker was a veteran in the missionary field and often visited with Bishop Whipple all the Indian stations. He was consecrated bishop of Indiana, in 1883, and died the last day of the year 1894.

There were others, a little later on—well worthy of mention—as Rev. Wm. C. Pope and the Rev. Mr. Tanner, who yet remain to witness the growth of a state and the Church from its infancy to a strong and vigorous maturity.

Such laymen as Henry T. Welles, Harvey Officer, Alexander Cathcart and Judge Wilder, whose voice has been eloquent in the highest councils of the Church for more than forty years, must not be forgotten.

These are the men who laid the foundations of the Church in the State of Minnesota. They were the men who followed quickly in the steps of Dr. Breck, and when he saw them all placed and the Church in safe hands for the future then he turned his face westward; pressing ever on lest the time would fail him, ere all the schools of the prophets should be established.

# CHAPTER XXX

## WAYS AND MEANS

How Dr. Breck secured the funds for his enterprises, must be the mystery and wonder of all readers of this history. I count it the peculiar glory of his life that he created a new era in giving for missions. Before him there was nothing, behind him he left an aroused people. He smote the rock with his pen, and the waters gushed out in abundance, and since that day the Church has enjoyed the awakening. In his day and time old things passed away and behold all things have become new. The Board of Missions gave him and his two associates $300 a piece, but this was a trifle to the new man at the front. He needed $10,000. He required as much for St. Paul and the Indian mission and Faribault and California, and he raised it all himself. The times were unfavorable, when he set out for the west. It was over sixty years ago that the work at Nashotah began. When Dr. Breck started westward that section of our country lying north of St. Louis and west of the Great Lakes was a veritable wilderness. Its highways were Indian trails. Its guideposts, trees blazed by the woodman's ax. Where now large cities flourish then only the log-cabin of the pioneer or the wigwam of the Indian marked the spot. One half the continent was unoccupied by the white man, in 1840. It was not until 1849 that California began to be the Eldorado of the gold hunter's dream. The East had few millionaires then, and the Church was weaker than the country, comparatively. There was little being done in the foreign field and even less for domestic missions. Dr. Breck himself was but a youth of twenty-two years, without experience and without financial backing beyond his missionary stipend of $300 a year. Others have endured as great trials and encountered obstacles requiring equal courage, but if a man in the wilderness attempts expensive operations he must be able to secure from some source and in some way the financial assistance requisite to his undertakings. Dr. Breck from the first addressed himself to this herculean task, and as he came east personally not oftener than once in nine years, we conclude that the pen was the power employed to raise the funds spent at Nashotah, at St. Paul, at the Indian missions, at Faribault and last of all at Benicia, California. There are some people who to-day discredit the power of the pen for raising money. True, the pen is but an instrument revealing a power behind it, and it is really this character behind that makes it effective. Faith with works removes the mountain of disability. The first friends of

Dr. Breck were also his last friends. Many who went out with him in their interest to Nashotah, followed him to California, and the secret of it all was that he made them partners of his work. He made himself to appear as the agent of others. His achievements in the field were their achievements. His success was their success. He kept alive and glowing the enthusiasm of his confrères by opening up new vistas to their ardent gaze. With their leader they were ever advancing to unknown regions and to new conquests, until they almost challenged him to ask more than they were ready and willing to give. Miss Edwards, the President of the Bishop Seabury Society of New Haven, with her friends, entered the mission field at Nashotah in 1843, and the sum total of their offerings from that time to the close of his mission life in California was upwards of $10,000, convincing evidence indeed of how loyal and devoted these noble women were to the great missionary. Mr. Schemerhorn of Pittsburg, Mrs. and Mr. Douglas of Rochester, New York, were always reliable. Mr. Sass of South Carolina enabled him to purchase 460 acres of land at Nashotah. Mr. James W. Aspinwall, his brother-in-law, was always his generous supporter. His devoted brother Charles Breck of Carlisle, Pa., was a right hand man. Dr. Breck's letters to him always began, "My precious Brother," reminding one of the friendship of David and Jonathan.

The list of regular contributors grew steadily, a lengthening chain, each succeeding year. A single instance well illustrates the faith of the man and the generosity of his friends. When Dr. Breck started from Minnesota for New York, the time was fixed and the day of his departure at hand, but he had no money for the journey of himself, his wife and children, and yet he did not hesitate to make his preparations. And it was only the day before he left that the mail brought him two checks from two friends in Paris of $500 each for the journey to New York. At Pittsburg there were $500 awaiting him from Mr. Schemerhorn, and a check of the same amount met him in New York from his friend, Mr. Aspinwall. In 1863–4, Dr. Breck came East in the interest of the Faribault Cathedral, and remained nine months. As a result of this labor he sent Bishop Whipple $11,313.51 which he had collected. "I have consented," he writes, "to all this night and day and Sunday toil for the past nine months in order that this work of the Diocese may be established at an early day, and I trust to reach Faribault for the early Easter morning service." And now one word more of his "leave taking" of Minnesota and the esteem in which he was held by those he left behind, and then we may start on the long journey to San Francisco.

Dr. Breck writes his brother Charles, May 28, 1867:

"I have now made my arrangements to leave Faribault June 17th;" but once more his heart turns to his Indian friends, and when he writes the above, he is on his final journey to St. Columba two hundred miles away. It would not be consonant with my purpose in this history to quote all the letters and resolutions uttered respecting Dr. Breck's departure for California. Bishop Whipple, the Press of Faribault, the Board of Trustees of the Seminary, the convention of the Diocese all expressed themselves on the occasion. The ladies of the Parish presented him with a gold watch in testimony of their affection. The language of the local Press is especially valuable, "Since Dr. Breck first made Faribault his residence, his labors for the Church to which he belongs must have been most zealous and untiring. He has done a work among the sick and poor which will never be forgotten by them or us who have been daily witnesses of his self-denying efforts in their behalf. In the times of contagious sickness or distress of any kind, he has been their never-failing helper and friend, often relieving their wants from his own purse; we can only grieve that duty calls him from us. We have no fears that he will not succeed in his new field of labor, for he carries with him the surest element of success, the earnest determination to do his duty in all things." We have no data on the subject, but about this time Dr. Breck married his second wife Miss Sarah E.

Styles, of St. Louis, who proved an excellent helpmate and stepmother to his boys and who survived him but two years; she died at Paterson, New Jersey.

It is not my intention or desire to weary the reader with procrastination in these final chapters. It requires but a hint to read between the lines and fill up with detail, when once you have the man and his work and purpose well in hand; but one must not think to find in Dr. Breck a "spent runner" at this point in his life, as California was to be his last venture, so it must be a strenuous one. Dr. Breck never set his face so like a flint as when he pulled himself together for this last venture of faith. "His eye was not dim nor his natural force abated," so he was and so he seemed if we may judge him by the intensity of his exertions and the splendid courage with which he entered upon the preparation for his mission to California. If I tell you that he delivered one hundred and twenty-five addresses in sixty days, that he gathered together a company of fourteen persons, organized them, provided for their transportation and shipped them for California, a country he had never seen, a land to which all were strangers in a few weeks, you will grasp the situation. On the evening of October 9th, the mission was organized in the Church of the Holy Communion, New York; on the 11th they sailed on the good steamer *Henry Chauncey;* on the 19th they were at the Isthmus of Panama; on November 3d, at sunrise, they were in the harbor of San Francisco; on Monday the 5th, they journeyed to San Mateo, California, sixty miles from the coast, where, singular to relate, they were met by the Rev. E. Steele Peake who was then Rector of Trinity Church, San José, and who had already erected a wooden building ample for the accommodation of the entire company. But before advancing we must repeat somewhat of the setting out and the journey by sea.

## CHAPTER XXXI

### CALIFORNIA

WE do well to note the fact that Dr. Breck made greater preparation for this journey than he had done for any of his missions. It was a great undertaking that he proposed for California. He gathered about himself fourteen persons, including the Rev. Dr. Merrick, who went with him to St. Paul twenty years before. There were young men of the ministry and candidates for orders, and matrons for the household. There was his family, a wife and two sons. No man of to-day would think of such an enterprise unless backed by a syndicate. At that time California had been settled for twenty years. There was a Bishop and clergy list of over thirty-eight persons. There were churches and congregations but there were no schools, and this was what Dr. Breck believed in. There was not a Theological Seminary in all the west beyond Faribault, and this fact was well known to Dr. Breck. He went to establish one to fill the void, to meet the occasion. Some have thought Dr. Breck mistook his mission, that he was taken by surprise, that he had expected the savages to meet him on the shores as he landed. Dr. Breck was well aware of present conditions and the only disappointment possible was that he might not receive the support for his schools that he had every reason to believe would be afforded him. "My object," he writes, "is to locate in some central and agricultural district of that vast region, place ourselves and work under the Bishop of those parts, and commence the education of young men for the ministry." "I ask, therefore, for these, my associates, both clergy and candidates, an outfit sufficient to reach the Pacific coast and when there, a shelter for our heads. Like great national ventures into parts unknown we ought to have at least a year's subsistence."

The formal organization of the new mission took place in the Church of the Holy Communion, New York, October 9th, 1867. There were present at this service the Rev. Dr. Littlejohn, Dr. Irving, Drs. Tuttle and Haight with Dr. Charles Breck; all of whom made addresses appropriate to the occasion. They spoke of the past, of Dr. Breck's work, of Nashotah, the mission to St. Paul, of the Indian mission, and of Faribault, in glowing terms and then of California and the Pacific coast. It was a real love feast, and a consecration once more to the work of one who while others praised and promised secretly in his own heart, relied on the power of his pen through which the Holy Ghost wrought to establish, strengthen and support the work given him to accomplish. On the following day,

Bishop Cox was present in St. Luke's Church when the Holy Communion was celebrated, and a stirring and eloquent address delivered by the Bishop. All this was indeed gratifying to Dr. Breck. In the evening he visited the General Seminary and addressed the students there. It is a singular fact that the General Seminary never furnished a man for the West except Breck, Adams, Hobart and Cole, and these did more to arouse the Church generally to the work of missions than any other instrumentality whatever. It always seemed a strange and unaccountable thing that they themselves should have exhausted the missionary spirit of the Seminary. It was on the following day that the goodly company set sail on the steamer *Henry Chauncey*, via the Panama route.

A letter to his brother dated October 14th, 1867, informs us that all was well with them, that they were off the coast of the upper part of Georgia, that they had a full service on deck to the evident delight of the passengers, and that after the service the children were taught, and at night there was again a service and sermon.

These were days when the tide of emigration still was westward. On this very steamer were over a thousand passengers. It is well to note the fact that the Misses Edwards of New Haven were present to bid him Godspeed, faithful friends to the last of the great missionary. It is from his letters to these missionary ladies that we are indebted chiefly for information concerning Dr. Breck, and to them he writes on board the *Henry Chauncey*. He speaks of the character of the weather, and the ladies, who have all been sick. Of Mrs. Breck he writes that "had she been Columbus she would never have discovered America with such seasickness as they enjoyed, he is certain."

The company was received at Panama very graciously by Mr. McGraw (and dined at his expense). He was secretary of the Panama Railroad Co. Services were held in the beautiful stone Church at Aspinwall, and great attention was shown the missionaries, doubtless in consequence of Mr. Aspinwall's influence and interest in the undertaking. Apparently the entire journey to San Francisco was on pleasant lines, with no sickness, except that of the sea which was unavoidable. Quite naturally a rumor of the coming of this large party created very great interest among churchmen. There was a gathering of clergymen and laymen with Bishop Kip at their head to meet the strangers, and when the weather-stained voyagers once more trod the solid ground they found awaiting them a cordial welcome. It is very evident that Dr. Breck, while not prepared for the demonstration, was nevertheless not displeased with the enthusiasm which greeted him. Bishop Scott of Oregon was exceedingly anxious that the mission should be established in his own Jurisdiction, and before Dr. Breck left New

York there was an option whether he should favor Oregon or California, but Bishop Scott was at this time on a sick bed in New York City. He had caught the fever in Panama on his eastern journey, from which he died shortly after, and so did not meet Dr. Breck before he started. California was not therefore a dernier resort, but a free choice for Dr. Breck. The first location selected was San Mateo, sixty miles inland from the coast; and within two months from this time the mission was permanently located at Benicia. Dr. Breck concludes that the achievement of so important an end in so brief a time can only be ascribed to a special providence. Here were buildings, furniture and everything to hand. "Benicia Institute" was a college complete when Dr. Breck entered upon possession. Its site was ideal; thirty miles away across the bay San Francisco was visible. The situation, the elevation of it, the fruit, the flowers, the furnishings all complete; how could he be otherwise than delighted. For this plant worth $20,000 he paid $14,000, the half of which the Diocese was responsible for, the other half he took on himself, and appealed to his friends in the East to help him. His faith was sublime, his confidence in his fellow-workers in the East was wonderful. He says, "The mission had a balance of its outfit money left which realized in gold $2,000, which we paid on this purchase and we look to the assurance of the clergy and brethren which were everywhere made us the past summer in the East, and especially in those solemn meetings on the eve of our departure in New York, that we should not lack sympathy and cooperation. It is a property well located upon the great inland water thoroughfare of the state and within thirty miles of San Francisco. The buildings are of brick and wood, and are such as we could not hope to erect in two years' time nor at a cost of less than $20,000. There were thirty-five acres in this tract of land altogether."

The Pacific Coast Mission has by this purchase a missionary home for its clergy and divinity students and we stand this day (if we except the Romanists) the first and only theological school which has yet been founded on the Pacific coast.

To his brother Charles he writes September 23d, 1869, "You will not blame me when I tell you of the great family we have, numbering in all over eighty souls. For all these I am held responsible; at the same time I have to teach daily, also take charge of St. Paul's parish, Benicia, and prepare sermons and lectures. Then I do most of the editing of the *Pacific Churchman*." As to the effect of the establishing of this school on the Diocese the following quotation from a layman will afford abundant evidence. This clergyman had been for many years a hard worker in the Diocese. After two years he writes, "I rejoice to believe and know that your labor and influence over Church education are being felt in the state. The ice is broken, the apathy is overcome and the current is beginning to move. It is slow but real. I see it wherever I go, and in quarters where it surprises me, you have no idea what a work was to be done when you came, or you would be doubly thankful. I had begun to fear the waters would not move in this generation but now I feel it in brain and bone." The facts were the entire Diocese had been aroused and set to work and was glad and thankful of Dr. Breck's presence among them. His coming was a day of great awakening.

Dr. Breck writes, " When we reached this coast November 3d, 1867, we did not anticipate the opening of a boarding-school for boys, short of two years. The rapid development of the educational part of the mission is as surprising to us as it has been gratifying to the Bishop and laity of California. We have ten students intending the ministry, and we have founded a school which will be a continual feeder to the Divinity Department. The grammar school has seventy boarders under an efficient corps of teachers.—N. B. At this time we have sixty acres of land and in real estate and improvements which may be valued at not less than $30,000; we board and lodge one hundred persons counting servants."

Here is Dr. Breck's testimony to the value of Church schools as such, " Whenever we plant a good school, the more Churchly it is, the better it is sustained."

## CHAPTER XXXII

### INFLUENCE AND DEATH OF DR. BRECK

I DO not think the influence of Dr. Breck for good, upon the Diocese of California has ever been appreciated. At that time and before that there was not a Church school in the entire Diocese; there was no rallying centre of educational influence; no church institutions. The Church had a resident Bishop and thirty-eight clergy, but no institutional life, no college or seminary or girls' school. For the supply of ministers they depended on a source 3,000 miles distant. Bishop William Ingraham Kip, D. D., was consecrated October 28th, 1853, eighteen years previous, and with thirty-eight clergymen in parishes and missions represented the Diocese. This was the clerical strength of the Diocese when Dr. Breck appeared, but there were no schools, there was no provision for the education of boys and girls, and this was an intolerable condition for any Diocese. This meant the abandonment of all that a Church stands for, in the way of education. The parishes were like strong men with nothing to do, sunk in selfishness and sloth inconceivable. It is impossible at this day to imagine the hopelessness and helplessness of such a condition. Individual clergymen and the Bishop himself were in despair over the outlook. The dominant idea of Dr. Breck was schools, as the centre and life of an associate mission. It was so at Nashotah; at St. Paul, which latter place he abandoned so soon as it became evident that no school of the prophets could be established there. When he went to the Indians the first thing was a school. The little Indian boys and girls were gathered, and the teaching began with them on a plank seat under the open sky, and that within a week of our settlement; so in California, Dr. Breck at once opened his schools.

It was a new day and a new thought in church life for that distant Diocese. There was a new breath in the air, a new wind stirred the branches and leaves of the forests. There was an "awakening of dry bones," as of old in Ezekiel's day.

When Dr. Breck first purchased the school plant for $14,000 at Benicia the Diocese pledged one half the cost, which certainly indicated a lively interest in the undertaking. They were glad of his coming. Their "Rip Van Winkle" sleep of twenty years was over. At his clarion call they sprang to the breach. They rallied instantly to his support, their funds were pledged, their boys and girls filled his halls faster than he could erect them. Dr. Breck was more honored in California than he had ever been before. He was invited to preach before the Convention of the Diocese, and his sermon was printed in the

Report of the Convention. He was elected chairman of the Deputies to the General Convention in Baltimore, and a second election would have been his had he not declined it. There was nothing within the gift of the Diocese he could not have had for the asking. In the seven years of his labors in California he raised and spent $75,000 on his schools, and as long as Dr. Breck lived they were successful and flourishing.

St. Augustine's College as it was named had a boys' school, a theological school and a school for girls. This last was the dream of his soul and the delight of his eyes, the crowning work of his life. "If we can educate the girls," he said, "we shall have the future mothers of the land" and "their children"; and it was while dreaming and laboring that he fell on sleep; God took him, in the very midst; when all depended on his single arm he sank exhausted with his "Labors more abundant."

> "Apostle of the wilderness on California's shore,
> Thy dauntless spirit fought and fell,
> Blood stained it evermore, blood stained it evermore, ah me!
> The scarlet poppies spring,
> Around the ruin of thy work,
> Reared on thy faith's strong wing."

So closed the strenuous life of one of the most remarkable men our Church has produced in any age; as the years pass he will be more appreciated and honored. I have thought the time had come when one who knew him should speak out boldly what he knew of the great pioneer; no one ever gets to know such men fully, or at the time. A great man is hedged about with mystery, one cannot understand the mind of a king, one cannot know a Shakespeare or a Napoleon, or a Washington. When a man like Dr. Breck creates his own environment out of any conditions, who calls to his aid forces that seem to have no existence, he is like a spider who weaves his web from his own vitals. We know not how it is done. We can only appreciate the result without understanding how or why it should be. We watch his progress and wonder and admire his genius, for this is genius, a combination of faith and industry and courage which vanquishes foes and overcomes difficulties, because it does not know that they exist.

For the last event in the life of Dr. Breck I must depend on the testimony of others who were on the spot, and who were privileged to witness the closing scene. It was in the midst of an evening service that his strength failed him. He had just preached his last sermon on the preparation of Christ for his own death, and doubtless he was much moved by his subject, being as he was at that time exhausted with overwork. At first it was regarded as a temporary fainting spell, but it proved the beginning of the end. He never rallied, nor could his strength be restored. They bore him to his home, where he lingered for a week, and then while he seemed to rally for a few hours he suddenly left them, at one moment his soul was in his eyes; he smiled and then the light faded and he was gone; but the smile remained as a benediction. Dr. Breck was always fond of children, and these kept his room fragrant with their floral offerings all through that blessed week. Always unselfish he uttered no complaint, that thus it must be, but lived his little remaining span as if it was a part of the endless life upon which he was entering. His heart was untroubled, he had no regrets, he expressed no anxiety concerning his work; sufficient unto the day were the events of the day, and the morrow was in the hands of God.

## CHAPTER XXXIII

### THE BURIAL AT BENICIA

*"From the Pacific Churchman"*

"THE funeral obsequies of Dr. Breck took place at St. Mary's church, Benicia, Cal. Bishop Kip and Bishop Wingfield, assisted by the Rev. Dr. Stubbs, of New Jersey, the Rev. Dr. Guyon, United States Navy, the Rev. Messrs. Chapin, Cowan, Flack and Monges of California. The church was draped in mourning. The bells in the town were tolled. The teachers and scholars of both schools which he had founded were present—and a multitude of sorrowing friends from the neighborhood and from San Francisco and adjoining towns, were gathered to pay their last respects to the memory of the great missionary. Many could not obtain entrance to the building, but stood outside under the open windows. Over the chancel window was a sentence of flowers,—'*Blessed spirit rest in peace.*'

"The opening sentences were read by the Bishops—alternately, and the lesson by the Rev. Dr. Stubbs. The ante-communion service was by Rev. Messrs. Easton, Chapin and Cowan; the sermon was by Bishop Wingfield, followed by

Bishop Kip, with feeling and appropriate remarks. After the close of the communion service, the mortal remains were lowered to their resting-place, under the chancel window of the church. Clad in surplice and stole—the appearance of his face in death as in life—was calm, peaceful, at rest, 'life's fretful fever done.' Upon the lid of the coffin lay two floral crosses, and a star and crown. The hands were crossed clasping a cluster of flowers, and so he rested for twenty years, 'waiting the moving of the waters,' and the rising tide of public interest which should bear him to Nashotah." This account of his funeral at Benicia is from the *Pacific Churchman* —of which Dr. Breck had been editor for a time.

The Bishop of Pittsburg, in his convention address, thus refers to Dr. Breck's death:

"There has been the death of a Presbyter in a distant Diocese which touches our whole church —for that Presbyter was a leader such as God gives, only now and then to any part of His Church.

"The Rev. Dr. J. Lloyd Breck—his prime of life not yet past—sank literally under his toils and cares for the Church and her missions, but a few weeks ago in Northern California. He was my mate and friend in early school and college life and the tie of affection was never severed. His bold, manly, aggressive missionary life for some thirty-six years has been the glory of our American Church. To many of us who have watched his course all these years it seemed as though this American Church of ours without Lloyd Breck at work in it was hard to think of. His example is one that young ministers ought to study well before they settle themselves down too easily and confidently to a ministry carefully made to cost as little as conscience will permit."

The General convention for 1877 says of him in relation to California—" At the head of an associate mission he landed there in May, 1867, and located at Benicia—founded St. Augustine college and grammar school, with a Divinity school attached—and this being established and given over to a Board of Trustees, he proceeded to found a school for young ladies—St. Mary's Hall. It was in the midst of this very successful work that he suddenly died, March 30, 1876, leaving a vacancy in the Church which no one has been found to fill."

## CHAPTER XXXIV

### TWENTY YEARS AFTER

The burial of Dr. Breck at Benicia, California, occurred in 1876. Twenty years after his remains were removed to Nashotah, Wisconsin, where they were recommitted to the earth, literally, "Earth to earth, and dust to dust."

At the time of his demise, Dr. Breck expected to be buried under the chancel of St. Mary's Church, Benicia, California, but then he saw as in a vision, a stone structure in place of the present temporary one and all things were to be as he had planned them for a great Educational Establishment. Alas! that his dream should never have been realized and that "decay's effacing finger" has written over his work there, disappointment. The spirit has departed and at some future day even the poor remains shall be removed to a distant grave.

This question of removal had been contemplated some years before, and a committee appointed to carry it into effect, which committee appeared to have expired with its birth, but when the matter came up again in the shape of a letter from one of the sons asking what was to be done

## Twenty Years After

about the removal of his father's remains, a new interest was awakened.

At that time also the writer received a letter from one of the sons stating "that if the Church did not intend to remove his father to Nashotah, then he and his brother would seek a place for their permanent burial somewhere in California." With this condition confronting us we had no alternative. If they were to be removed they should come at once to Nashotah. The necessary funds having been secured it was so arranged that the son should come on with them to Nashotah, arriving the last week in October and while the General Missionary Council of the Church was being held in Milwaukee. This is how it happened that so large a number of the Bishops and clergy were able to attend the recommittal at Nashotah.

It is readily understood that the Bishop of Milwaukee was the moving spirit on this occasion. His tact and sympathy left nothing undone that ought to have been done, nothing to desire by the friends of the deceased that his forethought had not provided.

It might be said with truth that the Convention adjourned to Nashotah in a body. They filled a special train. The remains were already there in advance and the son, the Rev. Augustus Muhlenburg Breck, was also there. The president, Dr. Wm. W. Webb, had looked after all the details—the students assisting him, and acting as pall-bearers. The people of the surrounding country and friends from a distance were there to swell the company that assembled to show their respect, and do honor to the memory of the great missionary. There were also relatives, daughters of the brother already referred to, with their families. There was Josephine Ackley and her family, and Mrs. Leonard, once Kittie Breck, and her brother Lloyd and his family, and others; I cannot name them all. These had known him in the olden time when they were children and now welcomed him with glad hearts back to the scenes of his earliest labors.

The recommittal and the ceremonies at Nashotah were a great function, the greatest perhaps ever seen in the West. The occasion was honored by the presence of fourteen Bishops of the Church, a very unusual number to get together for such an occasion. There was the Bishop of the Diocese, who had worked so hard to bring it all about. Bishops Dudley and Tuttle, and Coleman and Leonard of Utah. Bishops Whitehead and Williams (of Marquette, Mich.), Atwell and Gilbert, and Peterkin and Millspaugh and Talbot and White and Brooke of Oklahoma. There were two hundred clergymen present and one of these, the Rev. D. D. Chapin, had assisted at the burial of Dr. Breck in California, twenty years before, when there were two Bishops and five clergymen present. He was one of the pall-bearers at this recommittal, a singular coincidence.

The burial casket was placed in the chapel, at the chancel steps and at the foot was the kneeling figure of the son, the Rev. Augustus Muhlenburg Breck, who had guarded it all the long journey from the Pacific coast. The chapel was crowded, and outside a multitude waited in respectful sympathy until the service was concluded. Bishop Millspaugh of Kansas gave an eloquent address, which recalled the hardships and trials of the early pioneers, and especially the long journeys of Dr. Breck and his associates in Wisconsin and Minnesota and afterwards at Faribault, where he himself had been baptized and confirmed, and afterwards educated and trained for the ministry. Bishop Nicholson was celebrant, and he closed the service of the Holy Communion, with appropriate prayers for the sorrowing. Then the students took up the casket and bore it from the chapel to the cemetery a third of a mile away. It was a "home coming" indeed, and more like the return of the "weary wanderer in many lands," than a funeral service; we were all glad of the day and the occasion and sang in our hearts;—

> "Apostle of the wilderness,
>   With reverence we bring
> Thee home unto thy Kingdom,
>   As one would bear a king.
> As one would bear a king we lay
>   Thee on Nashotah's breast
> A king returning from afar
>   To her who loved him best."

It was a long procession with Bishops, priests and people. A strange procession, winding its way among the trees, with mingled emotions of grief and rejoicings, until all had gathered on the solitary spot of vantage ground from which the institution itself—and the lake beyond are visible, and there when the sun was low, and the gray October day was closing, Dr. Breck found, we trust, his lasting grave.

The final oration was pronounced by the Bishop of Missouri, who spoke as he only could have spoken of the great man who led all the missionaries of the west in their quest of souls; of him who traveling over boundless prairies, and through interminable forests set the pace, and blazed the way for all who should come after him even to the end of the days, and when the Bishop had concluded and the multitude dispersed, we left him to his God in the "hope of a resurrection and a life to come through our Lord Jesus Christ, at whose second coming in glorious majesty to judge the world, the earth and the sea shall give up their dead, and the corruptible bodies of those who sleep in Him shall be changed and make like unto His own glorious body, according to the mighty working whereby he is able to subdue all things unto Himself."

## "In Memoriam"

Since that day of Christian rejoicing and

hallowed remembrance there has been erected by the Alumni of Nashotah, a monumental cross to mark the place of interment and on the stone we read —

*James Lloyd Breck,
Priest—Pastor—Doctor,
"Jesu Mercy."*

And on the base,

*"An Apostle of the Wilderness."*

It was at Nashotah Dr. Breck's labors began, and it was eminently proper that there his ashes should rest, with others who had been his associates in the days of his early struggles. There Bishop Kemper was buried and his sisters. There Lewis Kemper finds a resting-place. Drs. Cole and Adams, and Mrs. Adams the Bishop's only daughter, are garnered there, and many others of Nashotah's graduates and friends, and there finally the great missionary himself finds sepulchre. "They rest from their labors and their works do follow them."

On the day of the funeral, and at the request of many, the following poem was read and is here given as a graceful expression of the sympathy of one who has all through the writing of this history expressed the liveliest interest in its success.

## "AN APOSTLE OF THE WILDERNESS"

Apostle of the Wilderness,
    With reverence we bring
Thee home unto thy kingdom,
    As one would bear a king.
As one would bear a king we lay
    Thee on Nashotah's breast
A king returning from afar
    To her who loves him best.


Apostle of the Wilderness,
    Thy soul's young courage sprang
Straight to the front, and through the church
    Thy Faith's clear clarion rang.
Thy Faith's clear clarion rang—God heard
    And blessed thy prayer and deed.
His doves with olives went before,
    His ravens came to feed.


Apostle of the Wilderness,
    True Knight of Christ's dear Cross,
Shod with the gospel of His Peace,
    No fear hadst thou of loss.
No fear hadst thou of loss, brave heart,
    Thy shield His righteousness.
The Spirit's sword—a-flame within,—
    God's kingdom to possess.


Apostle of the Wilderness,
    Priest, Gentleman and Friend.
The Savage met thy courtesy
    And loved thee to the end.
And loved thee to the end—with those
    Whom God allowed to share
The blessings of thy comradeship,
    Thy fervid toil and prayer.

GEN. THEO. SEMINARY
LIBRARY
NEW YORK

MONUMENT ERECTED AT NASHOTAH, 1898.

Apostle of the Wilderness,
   Nashotah's sons shall keep
The memory of thy blessed toil
   Until they fall asleep.
Until they fall asleep in Christ —
   When Angels guard the sod,
Thy monument shall be for aye,
   The living Priests of God.


Apostle of the Wilderness,
   Nashotah's heart could hold
No rest for thee,—thy eager feet
   Pressed where the river rolled.
Pressed where the river rolled. Beyond
   Unto the sunset's flame,—
Swept the glory of thy Mission,
   The magic of thy name.


Apostle of the Wilderness,
   Prophet, with faith sublime,
Who placed his flag on Future's walls,—
   And clasped the hand of Time.
Who clasped the hand of Time—and saw
   Beyond all human fears,
Beyond the deep morass of doubt,
   Beyond the toil of years.


Apostle of the Wilderness,
   On California's shore
Thy dauntless spirit fought and fell,
   Blood-stained it evermore.
Blood-stained it evermore,—ah me !
   The scarlet poppies spring
Around the ruin of thy work,
   Reared on thy faith's strong wing.

Apostle of the Wilderness,
  Forgive our disrespect —
Forgive our selfishness towards thee,
  Forgive our great neglect.
Forgive our great neglect—God grant
  The Church shall rise in might,
And build for thee thy cherished walls
  On thy foundation's site.


Apostle of the Wilderness,
  Star of the Western night
The Church within her jeweled crown
  Wears radiantly thy light.
Wears radiantly thy light. Afar
  In God's eternal sky,
They who turn soul's to righteousness
  Shine ever and for aye.


Apostle of the Wilderness,
  With reverence we bring
Thee home unto thy kingdom,
  As one would bear a king.
As one would bear a king we lay
  Thee on Nashotah's breast,
A king returning from afar
  To her who loves him best.

—HELEN HOLCOMBE DENTON.

# ADDENDA

## Note on Faribault

Unquestionably, in its outcome, Dr. Breck's work at Faribault was the greatest of all his works for education and for the Church in the West. Two things were accomplished by Dr. Breck in the nine years he spent there. First he built the cathedral and thus he made it possible to locate the Episcopate there, and then he laid the foundation of *Shelton Hall*, and brought James Dobbin there and made him the head of the boys' school, a position which he retains to this day, having made it one of the most successful of the Military Training Schools in this country. After the Bishop came there he went on and developed the schools which Dr. Breck had already founded. It is true that through Mrs. Shumway and other friends of the Institution, the Bishop raised large sums of money to erect buildings—several hundred thousand dollars being given by this lady or left in her will. To get any adequate idea of the greatness and magnificence of this plant one must visit the place, and only in this way can they even imagine the importance of the Institution or adequately appreciate the work of Dr. Breck in all its length and breadth. The work of Dr. Breck at Faribault was enough to occupy the attention of one man for life, but for Dr. Breck it was but one in the chain of schools and missions, with which he intended to join the East and the West in the bonds of the "American Catholic Church." It is told as an incident by Dr. Tanner, who has written up Faribault more fully than any one, having been a tutor and professor there from the first, that once on the occasion of a mud-walk of eight miles into the country to hold a service, Dr. Breck was passing an infidel's house, a rough old farmer of a type frequently found in the early days at the West. Dr. Breck was offered a drink of water and fell into a talk with the man and so won his confidence that on his return to Faribault he was again invited to rest a while, and before he departed was invited to visit the sty and shown some very nice pigs of a very recent litter, and upon leaving was actually offered one of the pigs if he could get it home. The pig was put into a bag and rather than stop the flow of good feeling on the part of the man, Dr. Breck shouldered his burden and trudged five miles to Faribault with the pig struggling and squealing all the way. The "pig story" was always popular in Faribault, as an illustration of Dr. Breck's willingness to sacrifice himself in the interest of Holy Church. When one recalls the stateliness and dignity of Dr. Breck he can well imagine the picture. No hunter of the West was ever more intense or interested or skilful in the pursuit of game, than was our hero in his hunt for the souls of men, whether in the wild shack of a woodsman, or in the mansion of the rich, he sought them out with equal diligence, counting nothing a sacrifice if he but won a soul to Christ. Dr. Breck was equally a priest and a pastor, and the whole radius of twenty-five miles about his central schools was the fold, and all the sheep within this large fold he knew by name. In season and out of season he was the indefatigable worker who was never weary in well-doing. The boy of sixteen at Flatbush, who was willing to go to the ends of the earth if only he might become a priest of God, is the same in mature life, in the wilderness of the West, where no sacrifice was great, and no duty irksome if only he may thereby carry home some trophy to the Master he serves.

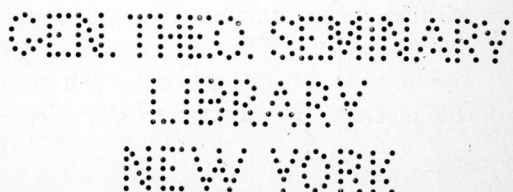

8237-4